Major Muslim Nations

TURKEY

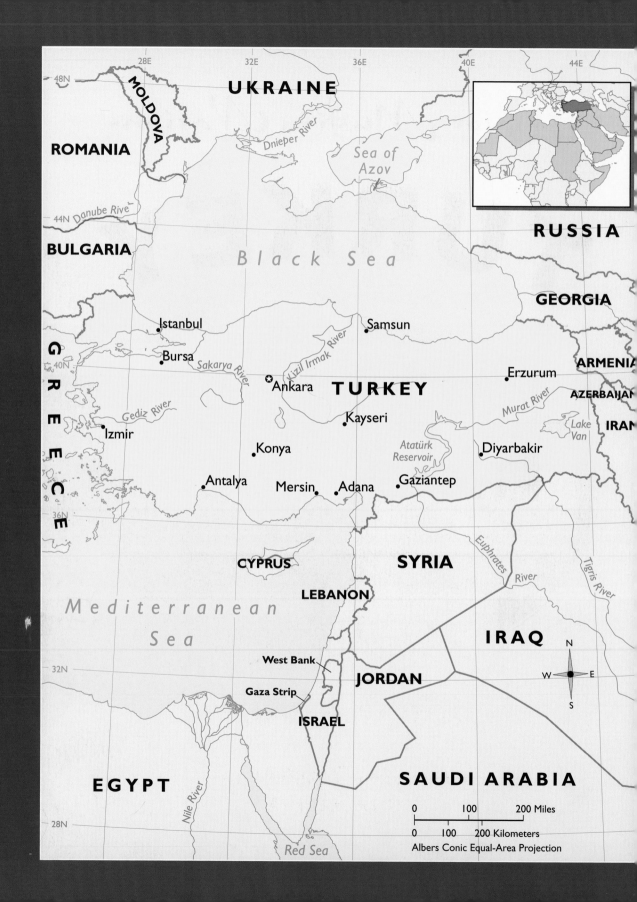

Major Muslim Nations

TURKEY

DANIEL E. HARMON

MASON CREST PUBLISHERS
PHILADELPHIA

Mason Crest Publishers
370 Reed Road
Broomall, PA 19008
www.masoncrest.com

First printing

1 3 5 7 9 8 6 4 2

Library of Congress Cataloging-in-Publication Data

Harmon, Daniel E.
  Turkey / Daniel E. Harmon.
      p. cm. — (Major Muslim Nations)
    ISBN 978-1-4222-1399-5 (hardcover) — ISBN 978-1-4222-1429-9
(pbk.)
  1. Turkey—Juvenile literature. I. Title.
  DR576.H37 2008
  956.1—dc22
                                    2008041234

Original ISBN: 1-59084-524-2 (hc)

Major Muslim Nations

TABLE OF CONTENTS

Major Muslim Nations

Dr. Harvey Sicherman, president and director of the Foreign Policy Research Institute, is the author of such books as *America the Vulnerable: Our Military Problems and How to Fix Them* (2002) and *Palestinian Autonomy, Self-Government and Peace* (1993).

Introduction

by Dr. Harvey Sicherman

America's triumph in the Cold War promised a new burst of peace and prosperity. Indeed, the decade between the demise of the Soviet Union and the destruction of September 11, 2001, seems in retrospect deceptively attractive. Today, of course, we are more fully aware—to our sorrow—of the dangers and troubles no longer just below the surface.

The Muslim identities of most of the terrorists at war with the United States have also provoked great interest in Islam and the role of religion in politics. A truly global religion, Islam's tenets are held by hundreds of millions of people from every ethnic group, scattered across the globe. It is crucial for Americans not to assume that Osama bin Laden's ideas are identical to those of most Muslims, or, for that matter, that most Muslims are Arabs. Also, it is important for Americans to understand the "hot spots" in the Muslim world because many will make an impact on the United States.

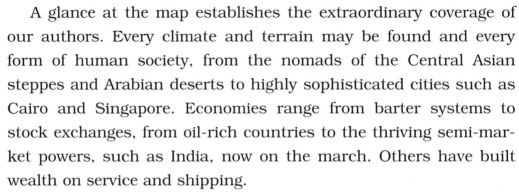

A glance at the map establishes the extraordinary coverage of our authors. Every climate and terrain may be found and every form of human society, from the nomads of the Central Asian steppes and Arabian deserts to highly sophisticated cities such as Cairo and Singapore. Economies range from barter systems to stock exchanges, from oil-rich countries to the thriving semi-market powers, such as India, now on the march. Others have built wealth on service and shipping.

The Middle East and Central Asia are heavily armed and turbulent. Pakistan is a nuclear power, Iran threatens to become one, and Israel is assumed to possess a small arsenal. But in other places, such as Afghanistan and the Sudan, the horse and mule remain potent instruments of war. All have a rich history of conflict, domestic and international, old and new.

Governments include dictatorships, democracies, and hybrids without a name; centralized and decentralized administrations; and older patterns of tribal and clan associations. The region is a veritable encyclopedia of political expression.

Although such variety defies easy generalities, it is still possible to make several observations.

First, the regional geopolitics reflect the impact of empires and the struggles of post-imperial independence. While centuries-old history is often invoked, the truth is that the modern Middle East political system dates only from the 1920s, when the Ottoman Empire dissolved in the wake of its defeat by Britain and France in World War I. States such as Algeria, Iraq, Israel, Jordan, Kuwait, Saudi Arabia, Syria, Turkey, and the United Arab Emirates did not exist before 1914—they became independent between 1920 and 1971. Others, such as Egypt and Iran, were dominated by foreign powers until well after World War II. Few of the leaders of these states were happy with the territories they were assigned or the borders, which were often drawn by Europeans. Yet the system has endured despite many efforts to change it.

A similar story may be told in South Asia. The British Raj dissolved into India and Pakistan in 1947. Still further east, Malaysia shares a British experience but Indonesia, a Dutch invention, has its own European heritage. These imperial histories weigh heavily upon the politics of the region.

The second observation concerns economics, demography, and natural resources. These countries offer dramatic geographical contrasts: vast parched deserts and high mountains, some with year-round snow; stone-hard volcanic rifts and lush semi-tropical valleys; extremely dry and extremely wet conditions, sometimes separated by only a few miles; large permanent rivers and wadis, riverbeds dry as a bone until winter rains send torrents of flood from the mountains to the sea.

Although famous historically for its exports of grains, fabrics, and spices, most recently the Muslim regions are known more for a single commodity: oil. Petroleum is unevenly distributed; while it is largely concentrated in the Persian Gulf and Arabian Peninsula, large oil fields can be found in Algeria, Libya, and further east in Indonesia. Natural gas is also abundant in the Gulf, and there are new, potentially lucrative offshore gas fields in the Eastern Mediterranean.

This uneven distribution of wealth has been compounded by demographics. Birth rates are very high, but the countries with the most oil are often lightly populated. Over the last decade, a youth "bulge" has emerged and this, combined with increased urbanization, has strained water supplies, air quality, public sanitation, and health services throughout the Muslim world. How will these young people be educated? Where will they work? A large outward migration, especially to Europe, indicates the lack of opportunity at home.

In the face of these challenges, the traditional state-dominated economic strategies have given way partly to experiments with "privatization" and foreign investment. But economic progress has come slowly, if at all, and most people have yet to benefit from "globalization," although there are pockets of prosperity, high technology (notably in Israel), and valuable natural resources (oil, gas, and minerals). Rising expectations have yet to be met.

A third important observation is the role of religion in the Middle East. Americans, who take separation of church and state for granted, should know that most countries in the region either proclaim their countries to be Muslim or allow a very large role for that religion in public life. (Islamic law, Sharia, permits people to practice Judaism and Christianity in Muslim states but only as *dhimmi*, "protected" but second-class citizens.) Among those with predominantly Muslim populations, Turkey alone describes itself as secular and prohibits avowedly religious parties in the political system. Lebanon was a Christian-dominated state, and Israel continues to be a Jewish state. Even where politics are secular, religion plays an enormous role in culture, daily life, and legislation.

Islam has deeply affected every state and people in these regions. But Islamic practices and groups vary from the well-known Sunni and Shiite groups to energetic Salafi (Wahhabi) and Sufi movements. Over the last 20 years especially, South and Central Asia have become battlegrounds for competing Shiite (Iranian) and Wahhabi (Saudi) doctrines, well financed from abroad and aggressively antagonistic toward non-Muslims and each other. Resistance to the Soviet war in Afghanistan brought these groups battle-tested warriors and organizers responsive to the doctrines made popular by Osama bin Laden and others. This newly significant struggle within Islam, superimposed on an older Muslim history, will shape political and economic destinies throughout the region and beyond.

We hope that these books will enlighten both teacher and student about the critical "hot spots" of the Muslim world. These countries would be important in their own right to Americans; arguably, after 9/11, they became vital to our national security. And the enduring impact of Islam is a crucial factor we must understand. We at the Foreign Policy Research Institute hope these books will illuminate both the facts and the prospects.

From the center of Antalya the fluted minaret, Yivli Minare, overlooks the Mediterranean Sea and the Taurus Mountains. Most of the people of Turkey follow Islam. However, unlike other countries in the Middle East region in which the governments impose Islamic laws, the Republic of Turkey has charted a secular course.

Place in the World

For many people, the land of Turkey conjures up images of powerful **sultans**, their lavish palaces full of intrigue, and of fearsome warriors wielding large, curved swords called **scimitars**. Such powerful leaders and warriors indeed existed. They wrote a bloody chapter in the country's history. However, they suggest little more about the true nature of this fascinating nation than a close-up photo of a boxing match or a graphic painting of a hand-to-hand Civil War battle would suggest about America to a foreign student. The people of Turkey today have much in common with the people of the United States. At the same time, they are unique. They have a fascinating history, and because of their location at the crossroads of dissimilar civilizations, they hold a very special place in the world community.

The Republic of Turkey—Türkiye Cumhuriyeti—is composed largely of a massive peninsula called Anatolia, which dominates the northeastern corner of the Mediterranean Sea. The country connects two continents: Asia and Europe. History has shown that its location, while vital to those interested in trade and conquest, poses unavoidable complications for its residents.

Turkey, with a population that is almost wholly Islamic, is part of the Middle Eastern world. However, it has had close links to Europe, both in war and peace. It was a German ally during World War I, when its northwestern coast was the scene of some of the war's bloodiest fighting. Later, Turkish troops joined Americans in fighting the Korean War. Today, despite changes and stresses in diplomatic relations, Turkey remains one of the most important U.S. allies in this turbulent region.

ANCIENT EMPIRES, MODERN INTRIGUES

The Anatolian Peninsula has been a land of empires from the time of the ancient Hittites to the early 20th century. As in other regions of the world, these empires rose, declined, and eventually collapsed, usually because of the combined pressures of weakened leadership and foreign invasions. Yet, two of them—the empires of the Byzantines and Ottomans—lasted many centuries. With the collapse of the Ottoman Empire in 1918, Turkey's age of empires came to an end. Sadly, the Ottoman system of government left the peninsula in a backward state compared with Western nations. The people of Turkey were ill prepared for the modern era.

During the early to mid-20th century, Turks were encouraged to modernize by their country's founding president, Kemal Atatürk. They opened themselves to Western ideas and eagerly adopted Western customs. Meanwhile, although they generally clung to their Islamic heritage, Atatürk insisted on freedom of faith and on a secular government, one in which religion would not have a controlling influence. In the world of Islam, **Sharia**—the law of the Qur'an (or Koran)—is expected to take priority over any government-made laws. The Turkish republic's attempt to separate Islamic law from the operation of its government has provoked opposition from many Muslim fundamentalists in Turkey and in other Muslim nations. This issue is more troublesome today than ever before.

Turkey has other serious problems. At various times since the 1890s, fighting has erupted between Turks and two minority groups—the Kurds and the Armenians—in the eastern part of the country. Hundreds of thousands of Armenians were killed and many more fled the country during internal warfare with, and persecution by, the Ottoman regime in the late 19th and early 20th centuries. The massacres of Armenians in 1915–16—which the Armenians have termed **genocide**—remain a contentious issue today. More recently, government forces have been sent to the Kurdistan region to counter violence by Kurdish rebels. The Armenian and Kurdish issues are complicated by the fact that neither ethnic group is confined within the boundaries of Turkey; their heritage and strong cultural ties cross national boundaries and thus lead to international entanglements and tension with neighboring countries.

Most tourists do not see the great struggle in eastern Turkey or the troubling religious issue. Their explorations focus generally on the "Turkish Riviera" along the Mediterranean coast and on other resorts, with interior excursions to visit the historic sites and observe village life on the Anatolian plateau. Without question, Turkey is an extremely interesting destination. It is a land of rugged and beautiful terrain, whose people are known for their almost excessive hospitality. A trip to Turkey is at once a step into history, a retreat to a vacationer's paradise, and an unforgettable adventure in regional cuisine, customs, entertainment, and world-class **bazaars**.

In this book, we will explore Turkey's geography, history, society, and customs. We will examine the issues it must resolve if its people are to live in peace.

Turkey is a country in which the ancient can be seen next to the modern. The city of Kaleici is a good example. Within the city, located in an area that has been inhabited for tens of thousands of years, can be found structures and monuments dating from the Roman, Byzantine, Seljuk, and Ottoman eras.

The Land

The modern country of Turkey, which is roughly the size of the state of Texas, occupies the Anatolian Peninsula in southwest Asia between the Black Sea, Mediterranean Sea, and Aegean Sea. Anatolia, most of which is hilly and rocky, was traditionally called Asia Minor. In this area scientists have found evidence of an advanced civilization that existed more than 8,000 years ago.

Turkey also includes a small region of southeastern Europe known as Thrace; it is separated from Anatolia by the tiny Sea of Marmara and the Dardanelles and Bosporus straits. Thrace, an area of green hills and grain fields, comprises only about 3 percent of Turkey's land area. But it is from here that the main part of historic Istanbul—Turkey's largest municipality—overlooks the Bosporus Strait.

Turkey's occupation of both coasts of the Sea of Marmara and the two straits gives the country a special geographic importance. It thus controls the single waterway that connects the Black Sea, with its European ports, to the Mediterranean Sea and the oceans beyond. The passage is as narrow as half a mile (0.8 kilometers) in the Bosporus. The broader Sea of Marmara is more than 170 miles (274 km) long from east to west and features islands where white marble is mined. This significant waterway has been both an advantage and a source of international contention for Turkey through the centuries.

Many factories have been built on the Anatolian side of the Sea of Marmara. The Aegean coastal region is Turkey's most heavily populated area because of its many natural assets. It has mountains and fertile, river-fed valleys ideal for farming. It has manufacturing centers. It also has fascinating historical sites and spectacular Aegean beaches that appeal to millions of tourists of many nationalities.

Ankara, the capital city, is located in west-central Turkey. From here, a network of highways reaches into the various regions of the country. They connect Ankara to Istanbul and to cities in Europe; to the Aegean port of Izmir; to important southern cities on and near the Mediterranean coast; to Gaziantep near the Syrian border; to Erzurum and other eastern cities; and to Samsun and Trabzon on the Black Sea.

The Republic of Turkey extends approximately 1,000 miles (1,610 km) from east to west and more than 400 miles (644 km) from north to south. In the Aegean Sea to the west, many islands lie just offshore. Although the north-south

The Turkish peninsula, historically called Asia Minor, is known as Anatolia. Modern Turks call it Anadolu. Their ancestors who conquered the land centuries ago knew it as Anatolé, its Greek name. The term refers to the east and means "sunrise" or "land of the rising sun."

Much of Turkey is rugged hill country. The Anatolia plateau rises above Turkey at an average elevation of about 1,640 feet (500 meters). The arid highlands are located between Turkey's two major mountain ranges, the Kuzey Anadolu Mountains to the north and the Taurus Mountains to the south.

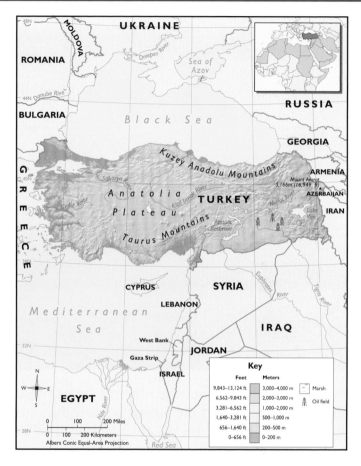

distance is only several hundred miles "as the crow flies" (straight-line distance), the jagged nature of the western shore results in more than 1,700 miles (2,736 km) of Aegean coast. (Remarkably, the Black Sea coastline in the north appears longer at first glance on a map, but it is actually 700 miles, or 1,127 km, shorter than the meandering Aegean coastline.) The Anatolian mainland rises from the Aegean to a broad central plateau surrounded by mountains.

Along the southern extent of the country, sometimes reaching to the very edge of the Mediterranean Sea, are the Taurus Mountains. Peaks in the Taurus range are as high as 9,000 feet (14,485 meters). The Mediterranean beaches of southern Turkey are noted for their white sands and turquoise waters; they are among the country's leading tourist attractions.

Mount Ararat looms over the village of Dogubayazit in eastern Turkey. At 16,949 feet (5,166 meters) tall, it is the highest point in the country. According to the Bible story in the Book of Genesis, after the Great Flood, Noah's ark came to rest on Mount Ararat.

Compared with the western part of the country, eastern Turkey is lightly populated. It is a region of highlands, lakes, grain fields, and pastures. Snow-crested Mount Ararat, Turkey's highest peak, lies in the eastern part of the country, in the area known historically as Kurdistan. Ararat is believed to be the site where Noah's ark supposedly came to rest in the famous story in the Bible's Book of Genesis.

LAKES, RIVERS, AND WATERWAYS

In the mountains not far from the Iranian border is Lake Van, Turkey's largest reservoir. It is a glacial lake of more than 1,400 square miles (3,625 sq km). Lake Van is markedly salty for a land-locked body of water and supports little wildlife. In all, Turkey has almost 300 lakes, but most of them are only a few square miles in size. Many were created during the 20th century to support hydro-electric power projects.

Also in eastern Turkey are the headwaters of the venerable rivers Tigris and Euphrates, which flow into Asia. In ancient history, they nourished the legendary "cradle of civilization." (At any rate, they formed one of civilization's "cradles"; modern archaeologists have identified others in China, India, and Egypt.) It was in

The Geography of Turkey

Location: southwestern Asia and southeastern Europe (the portion of Turkey west of the Bosporus is geographically part of Europe), bordering the Black Sea, between Bulgaria and Georgia, and bordering the Aegean Sea and the Mediterranean Sea, between Greece and Syria

Area: slightly larger than Texas
    total: 301,382 square miles (780,580 sq km)
    land: 297,590 square miles (770,760 sq km)
    water: 3,972 square miles (9,820 sq km)

Borders: Armenia, 167 miles (268 km); Azerbaijan, 5.6 miles (9 km); Bulgaria, 149 miles (240 km); Georgia, 157 miles (252 km); Greece, 128 miles (206 km); Iran, 310 miles (499 km); Iraq, 219 miles (352 km); Syria, 511 miles (822 km)

Climate: generally temperate with hot summers and mild winters; harsher in interior; most rainfall occurs during winter

Terrain: mountainous with a central plateau and narrow coastal plains

Elevation extremes:
    lowest point: Mediterranean Sea—0 feet
    highest point: Mount Ararat, 16,949 feet (5,166 meters)

Natural hazards: earthquakes, particularly in the north

Source: Adapted from CIA World Factbook, 2008.

the Tigris-Euphrates valley, mainly in modern-day Syria and Iraq, that the Sumerians—believed to have been the world's first civilization—lived more than 5,000 years ago.

Since independence, Turks have harnessed the ancient waterways by building dams. Most prominent is the Atatürk Dam on the Euphrates River.

The Kuzey Anadolu Mountains (also called the Pontus Mountains) line Turkey's upper coast along the Black Sea. In the northeast, these peaks rise to approximately 13,000 feet (3,965 meters). The world-famous Turkish tobacco is grown in the Samsun district, on the north-central coast. Farther east along the Black Sea, Trabzon is known for its hazelnuts. Northern Turkey is the rainiest part of the country. As a result, certain crops that require wet conditions, including cherries and tea, thrive in this region.

The Black Sea is an unusual body of saltwater, cut off from the oceans of the world except for the narrow passage through the Bosporus and Dardanelles. Much of its shoreline is steep and craggy. Several major European and Russian rivers—the Danube, Bug, Dnieper, and Dniester—terminate at its northern and western coasts. The sea's bountiful fish, especially anchovies, provide an important industry for Turkey and other nations surrounding it. At the height of the Ottoman Empire, from the 15th to 18th centuries, navies of the sultan dominated the waters; few foreign ships were allowed to enter through the straits and trade at Black Sea ports. Throughout Turkey's history, the confined nature of the Black Sea has affected its relations with other countries.

Besides the Tigris and Euphrates, Turkey's rivers include the Aras in the east; the Sakarya, which flows northward into the Black Sea from the west-central plateau; the Kizil Irmak and Yesilirmak in the north; the Seyhan in the southern Taurus Mountains; and the Gediz and Menderes in the west, flowing into the Aegean Sea.

A photograph shows the hilly coast of the Black Sea, a large inland sea that covers about 159,600 square miles (413,360 sq km). Important Turkish ports on the Black Sea include Trabzon, Samsun, and Zonguldak. Pollution has become a problem in the Black Sea, so in recent years Turkey and other countries in the region have increased their efforts to protect the environment.

FAMOUS LANDMARKS

Turkey is a nation particularly rich in historic landmarks. Across the country, it's estimated that more than 40,000 Greco-Roman sites still show evidence of those bygone conquerors. Latter-day structures also attract scientists and inquisitive tourists.

Turkey's best-known historical sites include the Cilician Gates, a narrow mountain pass through the Taurus range in south-central Turkey. It has been important for centuries to military operations and to travel and trade between the Turkish heartland and points south. Today, a railway through the pass links Istanbul to Beirut, the capital of Lebanon.

Another important archaeological site is Ephesus, a once-thriving seaport on Turkey's western coast that was excavated beginning in the late 1800s. Dating from the Greek period, Ephesus in the first century A.D. became one of the leading centers of Christianity in Asia Minor, largely through the teachings of the apostles John and Paul. Several miles from the site of Ephesus stands the Chapel of Meryemana, which some believe was the home of the Virgin Mary in her last years. The Arcadian Way, a street of marble, was built around the beginning of the fifth century A.D. to connect the harbor of Ephesus with the city's Greco-Roman theater. The ruins of the ancient theater, as well as the street, can be seen today. Ephesus was eventually abandoned after the various Arab invasions.

In northwestern Turkey, near the southern end of the Dardanelles Strait, lie the ruins of the legendary city of Troy. An ancient Greek epic poem, the *Iliad*, tells the story of a bitter war between Troy and the invading armies of Greek kingdoms. Whether the epic is mostly fact or mostly fiction is debatable, but Troy was indeed an important city in ages past. Actually, archaeologists believe that no fewer than nine cities existed on the site over a period of several thousand years. Some were demolished by conquering armies; one was ruined by an earthquake. Which of them was the Troy of Greek legend? Probably one of the latter cities, perhaps the sixth or seventh, which apparently fell to a Greek invasion force in the 13th or 12th century B.C. The last city located at the famous site, called Ilium by ancient Greeks and Romans, stood from about 300 B.C. to A.D. 400.

Istanbul, which occupies both sides of the Bosporus Strait and is thus in Europe as well as Asia, is one of Turkey's most fascinating sites. Founded by Greek colonists in the seventh century B.C. and called Byzantium, it later became the center of the Eastern Roman, or Byzantine, Empire and was called Constantinople. Ruins of the old city walls, built by the Roman emperor Theodosius in the fifth century A.D., still line the hilly Bosporus Strait.

The Hagia Sophia, or Church of the Holy Wisdom, brings together samples of the far-flung wealth that was controlled by the Byzantine Empire. Its sixth-century architects brought in columns from ancient Greek structures and Egyptian marble. They used ivory transported from Asia. The original Christian church became a **mosque** with the arrival of the Ottoman Turks. It is now a vast museum.

The Ottoman Empire's long rule can be seen in a more recent but highly popular tourist attraction, the Süleimaniye Mosque in Istanbul, designed in the mid-1500s by Mimar Sinan. The best-known architect of the Ottoman period, Sinan—the chief architect

One of the many famous landmarks of Turkey is the Hagia Sophia, which was built as a Christian church in Constantinople, was later converted into a mosque, and is now a museum. The building, constructed between 532 and 537, is considered one of the greatest examples of Byzantine architecture. The four minarets were added at different times after the fall of Constantinople in 1453.

in the court of Sultan Süleyman I—is credited with designing more than 300 impressive structures.

Also in Istanbul is the sprawling and splendid Topkapi Palace. Here the Ottoman sultan lived with his wives, children, court, and **Janissary** corps of soldiers. As many as 5,000 people occupied the palace at once. Many of its hundreds of rooms display magnificent Turkish rugs and fabrics, ornate fixtures, and gold furnishings.

In modern Turkey's mountainous central region lies the ancient region of Cappadocia. At one time a part of the Persian Empire, and later a province of the Roman Empire, Cappadocia features ancient caves and even cities that have been cut into the soft, volcanic rock.

SURVEYING THE LANDSCAPE

The climate in Turkey is generally temperate (neither extremely hot nor extremely cold). However, climatic conditions vary greatly from region to region. The central Anatolian plateau is a mostly dry region where surrounding mountains tend to prevent humid weather patterns from developing. In winter, temperatures on the plateau plunge. The eastern mountains are covered with deep snow for months on end, sometimes isolating the villagers who live there.

In the western and southern coastal areas, summers are generally dry and hot, while cool winters bring ample rainfall. The northern coast gets more rain. In the northeast, around the seaport of Rize, rain falls year-round.

Plant life also changes from one region to another. The central Anatolian plateau has grassy **steppes** and scattered woodlands. Parts of the great plateau are ideal for growing wheat, while cows, sheep, and goats graze in the grasslands. Some of the river valleys have irrigation systems that enable farmers to grow additional crops.

Coastal areas display a much richer variety of trees, shrubs, and flowers, and their fertile soil and adequate rainfall support agriculture. The northeastern coast near the Black Sea is Turkey's most fertile area. Oriental spruce, hornbeam, alder, and many other tree species grow in the forests there, along with shrubs that include laurel, rhododendron, and hazel. Common plants in the Mediterranean and Aegean coastal zones are wild olive, myrtle, and laurel.

In the rugged hills of Turkey roam bears, wolves, wild goats, wild boars, deer, hyenas, and other animals. The predator species pose a threat to grazing herds of sheep. To guard them, some shepherds rely on hardy dogs armored with spiked collars. Turkish bird life is plentiful and includes eagles, falcons, kestrels, and other birds of prey.

Besides sheep, goats, and cattle, farmers in Turkey also keep water buffaloes and camels. As in times long ago, many Turks depend on their grazing livestock to support themselves.

This unfinished Hittite monument in Fasillar, near Lake Beysehir, depicts a god standing between two lions. The carving is more than 24 feet (7.5 meters) tall. Turkey has been an important center of civilization and world history for thousands of years.

History

Anatolia was the homeland of the legendary Ottoman Empire—at one time the most powerful dominion in the world, in the opinion of many historians. But before the Ottomans, it was the land of the Seljuks, and before the Seljuks it was ruled by the Byzantines, who were preceded by the Romans, the Greeks, and the Persians. Before the Persians, as far back as the second millennium B.C., the Hittites held sway. But the Hittites were not the region's first inhabitants.

Scientists believe the first human occupants of Anatolia—later called Turchia and today Turkey—may have lived before 7500 B.C., during the Neolithic period. They planted crops, kept domestic animals, and lived in earthen huts. Archaeologists in 1961 found the remains of a Neolithic town in southern Turkey with buildings made of mud bricks. Relics included knives, jewelry, carvings, and wall paintings.

Early Turkish peoples are known to have fashioned a kind of cement flooring with inlaid marble and flagstone.

THE HITTITE ERA

A massive collection of early written records—thousands of clay tablets containing **cuneiform** lettering and **hieroglyphics**—was found in 1906 at the ancient site of Hattusas, near modern-day Bogazköy in central Turkey. The tablets date to the Hittite Kingdom, one of several kingships that occupied the peninsula about 3,500 to 4,500 years ago. In their time, the Hittites were the most powerful people of the region, spreading their dominion throughout the Anatolian heartland and southward into Syria.

The Hittites were noted bronze workers. They believed in various gods who controlled the forces of nature, as well as in local gods and spirits. At Hattusas, the famous Lion Gate—which still stands—was framed by monstrous, open-mouthed stone figures designed to intimidate evil forces. The Hittites enlarged the hilltop fortress of Hattusas, making it their capital. Its steep-sided, rocky perch made it a naturally protected bastion. The Hittites improved its defenses with a crude wall of huge rocks and a secret underground passage leading outside the city, through which their soldiers could surprise besieging armies.

Hawkish-faced Hittite warriors were bold and skilled, and their commanders were masterminds of battle planning and execution. Many armies of the day used chariots, but the chariots of the Hittites were superior, with spoked wheels and the capacity for two soldier riders. Few enemies could withstand a Hittite chariot assault.

Over the years, the Hittite occupation of Syria resulted in repeated conflicts with the mammoth sphere of the Egyptian pharaohs. Their epic clash occurred at the Battle of Kadesh in the 13th century B.C. Pharaoh Ramses II proclaimed an Egyptian victory, but some historians consider Kadesh a practical triumph for the Hittites. The peace treaty that ended the warfare between the two ancient powers left the Hittites in control of the disputed territory.

Only a few generations of Hittite warriors would revel in tales of glory at the Battle of Kadesh, however. Within a century, the Hittite Kingdom fell apart. Its society had fundamental flaws—wealthy, luxuriant cities were draining the resources of outlying areas, for example—and faced an assortment of eager invaders in waiting. It fell around 1200 B.C. to what chroniclers of old referred to as the "Sea Peoples." The origins of the Sea Peoples are unclear, but historians believe it likely that they came from the Aegean islands and possibly from the Anatolian coast. Ancient descriptions of these invaders undoubtedly are overly imaginative, but the terror they inflicted on those who lived in their path of conquest can hardly be exaggerated. They slew all before them and burned towns and cities to the ground.

THE TROJAN WAR

With the Hittites' decline, different Anatolian cities evolved into small kingdoms. This was about the time of the Trojan War, described in the ancient epics the *Iliad* and the *Aeneid*. The *Iliad* is attributed to the Greek poet Homer, the *Aeneid* to the Roman poet Virgil. Historians are unsure how much of the legend is based on fact. Certainly, the classic explanation of the cause of the war—a mythical dispute among ancient gods and goddesses—is merely fable. Nevertheless, a war (or perhaps a series of clashes over a period of centuries) apparently occurred between Greek kings and the city of Troy in western Anatolia. According to Virgil's account, it ended when the Greek army, seemingly defeated, abandoned its siege of Troy and left behind a token of respect for its worthy foes: the famous Trojan horse. Concealed inside the towering wooden

The wooden horse in the city of Canakkale is a reminder of the Trojan War, made famous in such ancient writings as Homer's *Iliad*, Ovid's *Metamorphoses*, and Virgil's *Aeneid*. The city of Troy existed near present-day Canakkale, at a strategic spot near the Dardanelles Strait. During archaeological digs in the late 19th century, the remains of nine cities were discovered, indicating that Troy had been occupied from about 3000 B.C. to A.D. 400.

horse was a small band of Greek warriors. After the unsuspecting Trojans laboriously rolled the gift inside their city gates, the Greek deceivers emerged from the belly of the horse at night and opened the gates. The Greek army poured through and destroyed Troy.

FROM THE "FARMER KING" TO ALEXANDER THE GREAT

Between the era of the Hittites and that of the Greeks eight centuries later, several notable civilizations thrived on the Anatolian Peninsula. Among them were the Urartians in the eastern mountains and early Greek settlers along the Aegean coast in the west. Another powerful group were the Phrygians. From the Phrygian era come some of the most famous folktales of Asia Minor. Among them is the story of Gordius, a farmer who became king simply because he happened to be in the right place at the right time. It is said that when Phrygian leaders decided their people needed a king, a fortune-teller told them to appoint the first person to ride past in a cart. When they looked to the road, they saw

Gordius driving his oxcart to market. He duly was made king, and the Phrygian capital was named Gordium.

According to legend, Gordius constructed an extremely complicated rope knot to attach the pole to the yoke of his oxcart. An oracle, or soothsayer, predicted that the person who could solve the Gordian knot would rule all of Asia, but the knot proved so complex that no challengers ever succeeded in untying it. Long after the death of Gordius, the story goes, the Macedonian conqueror Alexander the Great saw the historic oxcart with the legendary Gordian knot on display and devised an indisputable solution: Alexander sliced the knot asunder with his sword.

A different Phrygian king figures in another famous legend. According to the story, everything King Midas touched turned to gold. The historical Midas, who ruled about 700 B.C., never turned common rocks or wood into gold, although it's likely he accumulated substantial treasures during his reign. Within a century of the death of King Midas, however, Phrygia weakened and collapsed.

During the sixth century B.C., the Persians came to power in Anatolia, led by King Cyrus. There followed two centuries of invasions and counterstrikes between Persia and Greece across the Aegean Sea. They ended with the coming of Alexander of Macedon. In 334 and 333 B.C., Alexander won great victories over the army of the Persian king Darius III. Alexander's war machine conquered Persia, brought a lasting Greek influence to the Anatolian Peninsula, and swept far across the Middle East. After Alexander's

By the time of his death in 323 B.C., Alexander the Great had carved out a vast empire. His conquests spread Greek language and culture throughout the region.

early death, however, the astonishing empire he had carved for himself began to evaporate. On the Anatolian Peninsula, regional kingdoms developed and warfare became a way of life.

ROMAN ANATOLIA

In the second century B.C., the expanding realm of imperial Rome began reaching eastward into Anatolia. At first, the Romans came by request; the small kingdom of Pergamum in western Anatolia pleaded for their help in resisting the Seleucid dynasty of Asia. The king of Pergamum decreed that when he died, since he had no children to succeed him, Pergamum would become a Roman province. From this stepping-stone, Roman legions eventually took over the whole peninsula and established outposts deep into Asia.

Rome's sprawling domain, which extended from Africa to England, was divided in the fourth century A.D. The most famous Roman leader in the eastern part of the empire was Constantine. In 330 he officially established his capital at Byzantium, a city that had been built by the Greeks on the western side of the Bosporus Strait—the site of present-day Istanbul. The name was changed in his honor from Byzantium to Constantinople.

Constantine (A.D. 280?–337) became the sole ruler of the Roman Empire in 324; soon after, he decided to move his capital east. For six years, his workmen labored to transform an ancient city that had been founded near the Bosporus Strait in the seventh century B.C. by a Greek named Byzas. On May 11, 330, the new city, now called Constantinople, became the capital of the Roman Empire. Though the western part of the empire collapsed in the fifth century, Constantinople, as the center of the Byzantine (or Eastern Roman) Empire, remained a powerful and important city for another 1,000 years.

Throughout central and western Anatolia, the early Christian church had begun to grow during the first century A.D., despite horrible persecution at the hands of **pagan** Roman leaders and soldiers. Constantine himself became a Christian. He ended the bloody oppression of the Christians within his domain and built grand churches in Constantinople. Anatolia soon became a center of Christianity. Important church councils were held there during the fourth and fifth centuries, at Nicaea, Ephesus, and Chalcedon.

At the same time, Constantine was a brilliant military commander who mastered all enemies and brought enormous wealth to his capital. Constantinople, which grew to a population of more than half a million, permanently was established as one of history's great centers of arts and culture.

Roman leaders lived lavishly. They built imposing defenses around Constantinople to thwart the ceaseless threat of invasion.

In 395 the Roman Empire was divided into western and eastern parts. By the latter decades of the next century, the Western Roman Empire had fallen after a series of fierce assaults led by so-called barbarian warlords, but the Eastern Roman Empire (later called the Byzantine Empire), centered in Constantinople, withstood attacks from every direction and managed to survive into the next millennium.

ARRIVAL OF THE TURKS

In the 11th century, Seljuk Turks from the Asian heartland to the southeast began a prolonged invasion and settlement of Anatolia. These Turkish people originated far to the east, probably in the region of what is now

Turkey for many centuries was part of the Roman Empire. In fact, when the Roman Empire was divided in the fourth century A.D., the city of Constantinople—modern-day Istanbul—was made capital of the Eastern Roman (later called the Byzantine) Empire.

Mongolia. Livestock herders, they lived a nomadic lifestyle, constantly seeking adequate pastures and water for their animals, and living in tents made of goat hair. The ancient Turks fought among themselves for control of territory in which to raise their livestock. Over a period of centuries, various Turkish groups steadily moved westward, across the northern Middle East, in quest of better lands. Eventually, as they established themselves in new locales, they adapted to village life.

The Seljuks captured and looted the city of Caesarea (now known as Kayseri) in central Anatolia in 1067. They won a tremendous and conclusive victory over a Byzantine army in 1071 at the Battle of Manzikert. There the army of Sultan Arp Arslan not only destroyed the defending force but captured Emperor Romanus IV Diogenes. Within a few years, facing only weakened resistance, the Seljuks controlled the Anatolian central plateau.

The Seljuk hordes fought passionately for their Islamic religion. During two centuries of warfare against the Byzantine Empire, they forged a power center in Anatolia—although their influence never spanned the entire peninsula. Their domain was known as Rum (a translation of "Rome"), in recognition of the region's history as part of the old Roman Empire. To replace Roman splendor, the Seljuks established their own culture and grandeur in Rum, fostering master crafters, writers, and thinkers.

Seljuk expansion unnerved the Christian kingdoms of Europe. The Turkish threat was in part responsible for prompting the first of the **Crusades**, in the late 1090s. Four armies of knights, most of them from France, marched across Europe and united at Constantinople. From there, they swept through western Anatolia, recovering some of the cities that had been lost to the Seljuks, and proceeded down the Mediterranean coast to Jerusalem, which they successfully took from Muslim forces.

Over the next two centuries, the effects of the Crusades and

This painting shows the European crusaders after their capture of Jerusalem, July 1099. Two of the important figures of the early Crusades, the French knight Godfrey of Bouillon (arms raised) and Peter the Hermit (wearing the white tunic with red cross), are depicted near the center of the painting; around them are the bodies of Muslim and Jewish inhabitants of the city who were massacred by the invaders. The Crusades were a series of brutal conflicts from 1098 to 1291 between European Christians, who wanted to reclaim sites in the Holy Land, and the Muslim Arabs who lived there.

weak leadership were among the factors that spelled the end of Seljuk power in Anatolia. When the notorious Mongol hordes from Asia arrived, the Seljuk military was no match for them. In 1243 the Mongols slaughtered a Seljuk force at the Battle of Köse Dagh and plundered the cities of Kayseri and Sivas. Seljuk territory in Anatolia came under the control of the Mongol dynasty based in what is today Iran and Iraq. The Mongols controlled the region until their dynasty collapsed in 1335.

Meanwhile, the great Byzantine capital city on the Bosporus faced crises from other directions. The sheer numbers of the

This painting by the 16th-century Italian artist Palma Giovane shows Turkish forces attacking Constantinople in 1453. The fall of the city marked the end of the Byzantine Empire and the rise of a new power, the Ottomans.

crusading armies from Europe posed great hardships on the countries through which they passed, for the knights and their entourages devoured food stores and laid waste to crops. The people of Constantinople came to regard the crusaders as unwelcome travelers—even as enemies. In 1204 European soldiers of the Fourth Crusade diverted from their mission of attacking Jerusalem and instead laid siege to Constantinople. After a prolonged struggle, they captured the city, plundered its riches, and slaughtered many of its citizens. The brutal reign of the misguided crusaders lasted half a century.

BEGINNINGS OF THE OTTOMAN EMPIRE

From central Asia came another mass of invaders: the Ottoman Turks. Their most famous early leader was Osman. He and his successor sultans established one of the truly great world empires, which would last almost seven centuries. Ottoman armies in time conquered lands far away: deep into the Middle East, around the coast of the Mediterranean Sea, and across northern Africa as far as present-day Algeria. They pressed across the Black Sea to the southern fringes of Russia. They even invaded south-central Europe.

One of the Ottomans' first great conquests was the venerable city of Constantinople, in 1453. Solidly fortified, Constantinople had been subdued only once in history—when the rogue crusaders had taken it more than two centuries before. The Byzantine Empire was in its last years, largely alienated from the Christian kingdoms of Europe, which once had been its allies. Sultan Mehmet II managed to carry out a surprise naval assault that the Byzantines had thought impossible, and he combined it with a furious army siege. After seven weeks of fighting, the weakened defenders were overwhelmed. The longtime Christian capital became an important city of Islam called Istanbul.

SÜLEYMAN THE MAGNIFICENT

Süleyman I, the 10th Ottoman sultan, was known to his people as "the Lawgiver" because he revised the Turkish judicial system. To the outside world he became known as "the Magnificent." His empire was more lavish and mighty than any in Europe. His fleets of merchant and war vessels dominated all the seas touching Arabia and northern Africa.

Born in the 1490s, Süleyman was the son of Selim I (known to history as "Selim the Grim"). At the time of Süleyman's birth, Selim was the governor of the Black Sea province of Trabzon; he eventually became sultan. When Süleyman was only 17, Selim made him governor of Istanbul. In 1520, when Selim died, Süleyman was governor of the province of Sarukhan; he succeeded his father as sultan. Soon his armies were invading southeastern Europe and Arabian territory in the opposite direction. In 1529 the army of Süleyman laid siege to Vienna, the magnificent Austrian capital on the Danube River, but the Muslim forces were eventually repelled.

After the near-conquest of Vienna, Europeans lived in mortal fear of the Turks under Süleyman. One reason was the sheer number of Ottomans. Istanbul had an estimated 700,000 people—as many as the major European cities of Naples, Paris, and London combined. Another reason was the recognition that Turkish armies were much better disciplined and more dedicated than their European counterparts. A Flemish ambassador of the time, Ogier Ghislain de Busbecq, predicted that Süleyman's hordes soon would "fall on us with all the strength of the Orient. Will we be in any condition to face up to him? In my opinion, it would be sheer folly to believe it."

The dreaded conquest of Europe never came. Süleyman died in 1566, and his empire was beginning to weaken from internal problems. Rather than conquer the Christian countries to the west, the Ottomans were preoccupied with maintaining the territory they already controlled.

LIFE IN THE OTTOMAN EMPIRE

The Ottoman Turks spoke a form of Arabic and used the Arabic alphabet, writing in the right-to-left direction. Theirs was an empire of glory and great wealth. Ottoman Turks would leave a legacy of splendid creations, from beautiful handicrafts and cloth to magnificent buildings. The Ottomans did not require the people they conquered to convert to Islam. However, they relegated Christians, Jews, and other non-Muslims to a lower status. They imposed special laws on non-Muslims and required them to pay additional taxes.

Their sultan enjoyed perhaps the most luxurious lifestyle of all the leaders in world history, dwelling in huge, opulent palaces with countless servants and **concubines**. The sultan held undisputed power over his people. He could make whatever laws he wished, as

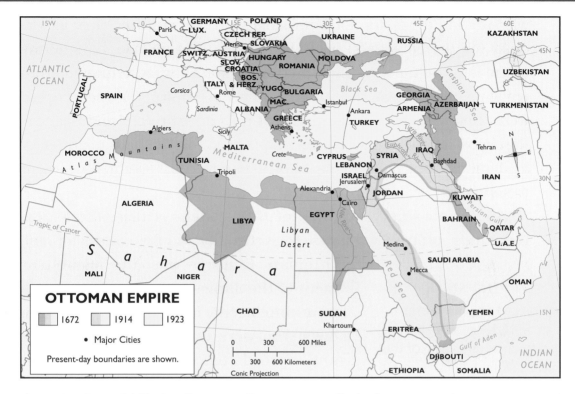

At its height in 1672, the Ottoman Empire controlled a large part of eastern Europe, northern Africa, and the Middle East. However, by the start of World War I in 1914, the empire had been reduced by the encroachment of European powers and weakened by internal corruption. The Treaty of Lausanne, signed in July 1923, established the borders of modern-day Turkey.

long as they did not violate the teachings of Islam.

Some sultans were only children when they ascended to the Ottoman throne. Once in power, they could have virtually anything they wanted—and their desires became extravagant almost beyond description. Believing that they represented God on earth, the sultans held a supremely vain opinion of themselves. They insisted that foreign kings and queens address them not by one grand title, but by many: "Sovereign," "Guardian," "Lord and Defender," among others. In return, they openly scorned foreign sovereigns as "infidels."

Among the first sultans, including Mehmet II, were remarkable leaders gifted not only with military cleverness but also with wisdom and a passion for knowledge and fine culture. They generously supported artists, poets, scientists, and philosophers. Many of the later sultans, on the other hand, were far more interested in enjoying themselves than in running an empire. So preoccupied were they with self-aggrandizement and unrestrained indulgences that most of the later sultans cared little for the actual duties of leadership. They delegated authority to governors—sometimes even to servants.

An extraordinary example of this system of delegation—and the kinds of predicaments it eventually would cause for the Ottoman Empire—was the establishment of the Janissary corps. Janissaries were intelligent, able-bodied Christian boys who were taken from their homes and forced to become soldiers. At Constantinople, they were converted to Islam and trained to fight. They were molded into one of the finest and most feared military legions in history.

This colored engraving from the early 18th century shows a Janissary, an elite soldier of the Turkish sultans.

Janissaries were not exactly the army of the Ottoman Empire. Rather, they were the personal property of the sultan. In this way, the sultan maintained total military control. He could rest assured that his soldiers would be loyal only to him, not to various Muslim army commanders who might plot rebellion. In a sense, the Janissaries were slave-soldiers. They were forbidden to marry or even to socialize with civilians. However, they were amply rewarded for their service. They received good salaries, lived in comfortable quarters, and enjoyed enormous respect not only from enemy armies but also from the Turkish people. They became no ordinary slaves. In fact, they enjoyed privileges unknown to many of the empire's free citizens.

The Janissary corps grew to as many as 200,000. Janissaries were made government administrators as well as soldiers. Eventually, some took up trades and began doing business with civilian customers. It was only a matter of time before their ranks became corrupt. Some offered their influence and services to enemies of the sultan. They began to exert power to suit their own interests. They could even control the fate of the sultans they served. Later sultans were terrified by these soldiers, who were supposed to be their faithful slaves. Janissaries made increasing demands, and whatever they wanted, the sultan usually ordered that it be given to them.

From the 17th to the 19th centuries, Janissaries staged several revolts against the Ottoman sultans. In 1622, before Sultan Osman II could carry out plans to eliminate the Janissary corps, the soldiers killed him and replaced him with a more amenable sultan. The Janissary era did not end until 1826, when professional soldiers organized and trained to serve Sultan Mahmud II put down a Janissary revolt and burned the mutineers to death in their barracks. The Ottoman army was reorganized—but it would be too late to save an empire in mortal decline.

LAST OF THE SULTANS

During the 1600s, the Ottoman Empire gradually dwindled in size and influence. Inevitably, outside powers began to chip away at its territories. By the 1850s, the Turkish sultan—and the Ottoman Empire he represented—was being ridiculed as "the Sick Man of Europe."

In some instances, the sultan literally was a sick man. When a sultan died, his sons—often many offspring born by different wives—frequently became embroiled in bloody fights not just to inherit the throne, but simply to survive. Through intrigues and secret alliances, one of the descendants would emerge as the new sultan. His brothers and half-brothers would be ruthlessly slaughtered or sent into lifetime confinement in a sinister building known as the Kafes—"the Cage." Sometimes the new sultan would die and one of the imprisoned rivals would become sultan, despite the fact that he was completely incompetent to rule and might even be insane.

Probably the most astonishing example was Sultan Ibrahim. In 1640 he succeeded his brother to the throne at age 24, having spent 22 of his years in the Kafes. He abused his harem unmercifully, laced his beard with diamonds, and became so fond of the soft, dark fur of sables that he dressed not only himself, but also his royal cats, in sable cloaks. He once stabbed his seven-year-old son Mahomet in the face for making a clever remark. His final, incredible excess was having his entire harem—almost 300 women—drowned in the Bosporus Strait. Shortly afterward, Janissaries strangled Ibrahim to death.

One of the last sultans was Abdul Hamid II, who ascended to power in 1876 at the age of 34. In some ways, he made efforts to cure "the Sick Man of Europe." He briefly established a parliament and drafted a constitution for the Ottoman Empire, offering his people fleeting hope that they might have some voice in government. Those gestures proved insincere, though. And Abdul Hamid turned out to be as ruthless as most of his predecessors. He authorized the army to slaughter an estimated 300,000 Armenians in 1895–96 because he feared that the Armenians, supported by European governments, were plotting revolution.

In the coming years, many Turkish military officers who were sent to Europe for training came to realize the limitations of their homeland's government, particularly its repressiveness. Joined by restless students, they began organizing secret political groups to plot an end to the sultans' rule. Rising to prominence among these dissenters in 1907–08 was the Committee of Union and Progress (CUP), or "Young Turks." The group gained the backing of the Ottoman army, successfully demanded that Abdul Hamid approve a national constitution, and in 1909 forced Abdul from power. His brother Mehmet V succeeded him as sultan but was virtually powerless. The Young Turks effectively controlled the Ottoman Empire—if only for a brief moment.

KEMAL ATATÜRK AND INDEPENDENCE

World War I, which broke out in 1914, brought not just the defeat of the Ottoman Empire, but its total collapse. At its high point, the empire had reached well into the European continent and, in the other direction, almost all the way around the Mediterranean coast. By the end of the First World War in 1918, Ottoman territory was confined basically to the area of modern-day Turkey.

Ottoman Turkey sided with Germany in the world war—and lost. The "Sick Man of Europe," crushed by relentless enemies on all sides during the conflict, effectively went to his death by surrendering in October 1918. The victors were England, France, the United States, and Italy. It appeared that they and their allies, including Greece, would divide Turkey into several different states and provinces. But one Turkish leader had a different idea. His name was Mustafa Kemal.

Mustafa (the nickname Kemal, meaning "perfection," would later be given to him by a teacher) was born in 1881 in Salonika (present-day Thessaloníki, Greece). His father died when the boy was seven years old. Although his mother urged him to acquire a Muslim education and become a religious leader, he decided instead to join the army. On his own, he broadened his knowledge by studying literature, history, and social issues and learning German and French.

One of the leaders of the Young Turks, Kemal served heroically as a military officer in World War I. But his defining role lay ahead. In August 1920, two years after the world war had ended, the victorious nations crafted the Treaty of Sèvres. Its terms were unbearably harsh toward the Ottomans. In fact, among other measures the treaty called for the abolition of the Ottoman Empire, a separate Armenia, and Greek control of both sides of the Dardanelles. While the defeated sultan was obliged to accept the terms, thousands of angry Turks, especially young people, were uniting for an independent nation.

Bent on quashing nationalist resistance to the treaty, Greek forces invaded the ravaged Ottoman heartland from the west. Kemal was appointed commander of one of the Turkish defending forces. His ambitions went far beyond merely driving off the Greeks, though. His dream was to forge a new Turkish nation with its own congress and constitution, shake off the Ottoman past once and for all, and rid Anatolia of European occupation forces and invaders.

Over a period of three years, Kemal's nationalists succeeded. After a desperate struggle, his forces stopped the invading Greek army at the Sakarya River, then quickly drove them back to the Aegean coast. The Greeks ignobly returned home across the sea, and Kemal shifted his focus from military power to international politics. He made terms with France and Italy, resulting in the removal of their occupation forces. That left only the British, who occupied Constantinople. England did not want a new war. With the Treaty of Lausanne in 1923, the European powers accepted Turkey as an independent new nation. Kemal became the nation's first president.

Although he had led Turkey to independence from foreign—notably Western—control, Kemal was by no means opposed to

Western ideas. In fact, he believed that adoption of Western political and social models would be necessary to bring Turkey into the modern world. More than anything, he was determined to eliminate the vestiges of Ottoman influence. Even before the Treaty of Lausanne was signed, Kemal had done away with the historic line of sultans, who for centuries had ruled the Ottoman Empire. In 1924 he abolished the revered position of **caliph** (Islamic leader) and soon ordered the closure of religious schools. These moves—astounding in the overwhelmingly Muslim country—signaled not only Kemal's insistence on separating religion from state matters, but also his goal of reducing Islam's influence in Turkish society in general. In the political realm, the new Turkish constitution gave

Turkish president Mustafa Kemal Atatürk at a formal occasion in Ankara, 1934. During the First World War, Atatürk led the Turkish military in resisting an invasion by a combined British-French force in 1915; the Gallipoli campaign was a disaster for the Allies. After the war Atatürk successfully led Turkey to independence; during his 15-year presidency he instituted many reforms and changes.

ultimate power to a legislative body, the Grand National Assembly, effectively ending Islam's role in government.

Kemal took many steps to modernize his nation. He spearheaded Turkey's adoption of new legal codes. He outlawed the old practice of polygamy, or multiple marriage, and gave women the right to vote. He replaced the Arabic lettering that had been used during the Ottoman era with a modified version of the Latin alphabet, which forms the basis of the alphabets in use in Western nations. He had Turkey abandon the Islamic lunar calendar and adopt the Gregorian calendar.

Other reforms swept away old traditions. For example, Kemal forbade men to wear the **fez**, a flat, brimless hat common in some Arab countries. He said women no longer needed to veil their faces—a long-standing Islamic custom.

Kemal's influence on the development of modern Turkey can hardly be overstated. Independent Turkey adopted a **republican** form of government (though, it must be noted, the only legal political party was Kemal's Republican People's Party, known by its Turkish acronym, CHP), but historians in time came to refer to Turkey's unique government system during the 1920s and 1930s as "Kemalism." So revered was Mustafa Kemal among his people that in 1934 the Grand National Assembly bestowed on him the surname by which he is known today: Atatürk, meaning "Father of the Turks."

From its early years, Turkey differed in one critical aspect from many of its neighbors in the Middle East (and the Third World in general). Whereas Syria, Lebanon, Iraq, Jordan, Algeria, Tunisia, and Libya were all administered by European powers such as France and Great Britain, under Kemal Atatürk, Turkey successfully avoided foreign control. Yet Kemal was noted basically as a man of peace. After securing Turkey's independence, his focus was on modernizing his country and educating his people.

WORLD WAR II AND BEYOND

Soon after Atatürk's death in 1938, World War II erupted. The conflict eventually involved fighting in Europe, North Africa, and Asia and pitted the so-called Axis nations (Germany, Italy, and Japan) against the Allies (principally Great Britain, the Soviet Union, the United States, and France). Having suffered defeat and near-dismemberment by joining the losing side in the first global war, Turkey naturally refrained from openly allying itself with either side in the second. Unofficially, it aided the Allied powers, but it did not formally declare war against Germany until a few months before the war's end in 1945. By that time, the outcome of the war had been decided.

A man wears traditional dress, including a fez, in Turkey.

After the war, Turkey cultivated strong ties with the United States. It also adopted a multiparty political system. Yet the path toward greater openness and democracy hasn't always been smooth. In fact, during the last half of the 20th century the Turkish military intervened in the nation's political affairs three times—in 1960, 1971, and 1980. Three years after the 1980 coup, the armed forces once again yielded control of Turkey's government, and while civilian authority has prevailed through the early years of the 21st century, disquieting issues remain.

A Turkish rug maker chooses silk for a carpet in Hereke, Turkey. The textile industry is an important part of Turkey's economy, which is one of the strongest and most diverse in the Middle East.

The Economy, Religion and Politics

Though Turkey emerged from the Ottoman period as an independent nation, it lagged far behind the developed countries of the West. The European continent, to whose coattails it clung, long before had entered headlong into the industrial era, whereas Turkey had only basic factories and mills to process its raw materials. The Ottoman sultans had managed to keep their empire together for many centuries, but they had cared little for the common people. To make matters worse, World War I had ravaged the Turkish population and the economy. "Our country is completely in ruins," stated Kemal Atatürk in the wake of World War I and at the beginning of Turkey's three-year struggle for independence. "We have not one city left that people can live in. . . . We have no roads. Our people are poor, ignorant and miserable."

The new republic had only 2,500 miles (4,023 km) of rail

line (all of it owned by foreign companies) and almost no paved roads. It owed vast sums to foreign investors who had loaned funds to the sultans. Peasant farmers were so heavily taxed and over-charged for seeds and essentials that they never got out of debt.

Atatürk was determined to modernize his new country—and his early achievements made a remarkable beginning. Under his leadership industry began to expand. Perhaps the main asset Kemal gave his people, though, was a new vision: the notion that the young nation could progress in peace, that the Turkish people's lot in life could improve, that they had a leader who understood them.

A look at conditions in present-day Turkey illustrates just how far the country has come in its 85 years as an independent state.

EDUCATION

Turks are comparatively literate people. Under President Atatürk, basic education became available to all Turkish young-sters at no cost. Atatürk established a national Ministry of Education to oversee education standards for all students. Today, about 88 percent of the population can read and write. This is a remarkably high rate, especially considering that almost no Turkish villagers at the time of independence could read or write. Among his other initiatives, Atatürk promoted primary education in rural areas.

A 16-year-old student looks over his papers in a chemistry class, Istanbul. The Turkish gov-ernment has stressed education for all of its citizens.

The symbols on the Turkish flag—crescent and five-pointed star—are traditional Islamic symbols. This form of the flag dates to 1844, when it was adopted by the Ottoman rulers; when the empire dissolved and the Republic of Turkey was created, it became the national flag.

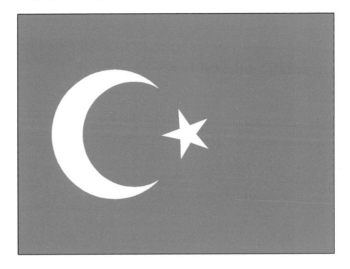

School attendance—which is required for youths up to age 15—is higher than 95 percent. Pupils are taught not only reading, math, science, and history, but also geography, art, and music. Many students go on to technical and vocational schools and universities. Turkey today has more than 70 universities, almost four times as many as it had just 20 years ago. Most of the largest, oldest, and most prestigious universities are in Istanbul and Ankara.

Academic training prepares Turks for a variety of modern careers. Many are employed in technology, manufacturing, and other professions. Meanwhile, others carry on the ancient and respected trades of their ancestors: handcrafting carpets and other items, selling wares in street stalls, raising crops and livestock.

ECONOMIC OVERVIEW

From the impoverished and underdeveloped land that staggered to independence in 1923, Turkey has since emerged as an economically diversified, relatively prosperous nation (though it still faces significant economic problems). As of 2007, Turkey could claim the world's 17th-largest economy, according to the World Bank, an international development-assistance organization. Estimates of Turkey's 2007 ***gross domestic product (GDP)***—the total value of goods and services produced in the country annual-ly—topped $657 billion. And per capita, Turkey's people fall into the middle-income range worldwide.

Industry employs about one-fourth of Turkey's workforce and contributes more than 28 percent of its GDP. The leading indus-tries are textiles and food processing. Approximately one-third of all factory jobs in Turkey are textile-related, and fabrics and processed leather goods account for some 70 percent of the nation's exports. Turkey also has an active shipbuilding industry.

Of the remaining exports, processed food items are the most significant. Cereal grains (most notably wheat) and sugar are important farm crops—though cotton is the leading export crop. Other export crops include citrus fruits, tobacco, potatoes, grapes, and tomatoes. Cash crops include sugar beets, sunflower, sesame, olives, and linseed. Around the western hill city of Afyon, beautiful fields of poppies flourish in season, providing a significant income for local farmers. Poppies are the source of opium, a drug that has medical uses but is also used to make the illegal drug heroin. In the 1960s and 1970s, most of the illegal opium in the United States came from Afyon. At the urging of U.S. officials, Turkey tem-porarily suspended poppy growing. When cultivation was resumed, it was regulated closely by the Turkish government to ensure that the opium would be sold only to the pharmaceutical industry.

About 36 percent of Turkey's labor force works in agriculture, although farming yields less than 10 percent of the country's GDP. A significant number of Turkish workers also produce ceramics and glassware.

Turkey is not a major source of petroleum, but because of its location it plays a role in the distribution of Middle Eastern oil to world markets. A vital pipeline that carries Iraqi crude oil through southern Turkey to the Mediterranean coast generates significant revenue for the republic.

Copper has been mined in Asia Minor since ancient times. Turkey's central plateau also contains substantial quantities of bauxite, manganese, sulfur, chromium, and other minerals. Most of the world's supply of boron is mined in Turkey. Boron, an element used to improve the quality of industrial metals, is one of several rare minerals found here; others include tungsten and cinnabar. Metal, cement, and chemical production are important Turkish industries.

The Economy of Turkey

Gross domestic product (GDP*): $657.091 billion

GDP per capita: $12,350 (2001 est.)

Inflation: 8.8%

Natural resources: chemicals and metals, including antimony, mercury, coal, gold, barite, borate, celestite, magnesite, copper, chromium, sulfur, iron ore, and copper; also water power, arable land, stone, clay

Agriculture (8.9% of GDP): tobacco, cotton, grain, olives, sugar beets, pulse, citrus; livestock

Industry (28.3% of GDP): textiles, food processing, autos, mining (coal, chromite, copper, boron), steel, petroleum, construction, lumber, paper, electronics

Services (62.8% of GDP): government, banking, tourism

Foreign trade:

Imports—$162.1 billion: machinery, chemicals, fuel, transportation equipment , semi-finished goods

Exports—$115.3 billion: clothing, food products, textiles, metal products, and automotive products

Currency exchange rate: 1.2785 new Turkish liras = U.S. $1 (Sept. 2008)

*GDP = the total value of goods and services produced annually.
All figures are 2007 estimates unlesss otherwise indicated.
Sources: CIA World Factbook, 2008; World Bank; Bloomberg.com.

Peasant women weed poppy fields in the Afyon region of central Turkey. Turkey and India are the only countries in the world in which it is legal to process opium from poppies. Opium, an addictive narcotic drug, has some medical uses, and the government strictly controls the official processing plants. However, illicit cultivation is also widespread, and opium can be processed into heroin, a dangerous illegal drug.

One economic advantage Turkey has over some other countries in the region is that most of its labor force has at least a basic education. By contrast, Libya, for example, has been forced to bring in foreign workers for certain higher-level—and higher-paying—jobs. An even greater advantage Turkey enjoys is its strategic location, which affords easy access to markets in all directions: on the Balkan Peninsula (Greece, Bulgaria, and other southern European countries), in eastern Europe, in the Caucasus states (the lower territories of the former Soviet Union), in the Middle East, and even in northern Africa.

Turkey's main trading partner is Germany. The United Kingdom and Italy represent its second and third most active trade partnerships. A fast-growing commercial relationship with Russia began to develop in the early 1990s, after the breakup of the Soviet Union. Generally, Turkey has strengthened its economic and political relations with the Central Asian countries of the former Soviet Union, where people of Turkic languages are dominant. Turkish investors are involved in construction and trade projects in Central Asia and the Balkan countries. In the Caucasus to the northeast, Turkey has excellent relations with neighboring Georgia and Azerbaijan.

ECONOMIC DIFFICULTIES

At the same time, Turkey's economy faces formidable challenges. Because much of Turkey is an extremely rugged land, transportation and communication systems are not easy to develop and maintain. Hindering improvement has been the country's history of sometimes shaky leadership and government corruption.

Not everyone in Turkey enjoys a comfortable standard of living. At the beginning of the 21st century, the most prosperous fifth of Turkey's people had an average annual income of more than $8,000 each, while the poorest fifth of the population earned, on average, slightly over $700—which works out to less than $2 per day.

In 2001 inflation—the increasing cost of goods in the economy—ran to nearly 70 percent. By 2007 it had fallen to about 9 percent, but 1 of every 10 Turkish workers remained unemployed.

A large part of Turkey's economic problems can be attributed to its huge national debt. Interest payments on this debt consumed half of all spending by Turkey's central government in 2001, which discouraged additional foreign investment in the Turkish economy. Adding to the problems were a banking crisis and a growing trade imbalance—the value of Turkey's imports exceeded that of its exports.

Another major drain on the Turkish economy was the 15-year-long war with Kurdish insurgents in the southeastern part of the country. That struggle, examined in depth later, cost Turkey billions of dollars annually between the mid-1980s and the late 1990s. The Gulf War of 1991, in which an international coalition led by the United States ousted Iraq from Kuwait, also hit Turkey hard economically. Before its leader, Saddam Hussein, invaded Kuwait, Iraq had been Turkey's second-largest trading partner.

A UNIQUE MUSLIM NATION

By the fourth century A.D., Christianity was firmly established in much of the previously pagan Anatolian Peninsula. With the coming of the Turks 1,000 years later, Islam replaced Christianity as the dominant religion. The change was gradual, as Turkish rulers gave churches and property to Islamic leaders and as Muslims and Christians intermarried.

The term *Islam* means "submission" in Arabic. Muslims profess their submission to Allah (the Arabic name for God). They follow the teachings of Muhammad, who they believe was Allah's last and greatest prophet.

Muhammad was born in Mecca, located in modern-day Saudi Arabia, around A.D. 570. After receiving revelations from an angel of Allah, he spent more than 20 years teaching a growing band of followers the things he said Allah had revealed to him. Ultimately these teachings were collected into the Qur'an (also spelled Koran), which is to Muslims what the Bible is to Christians. Muslims believe the Qur'an is written in Allah's own words, revealed through Muhammad.

Islam holds that Allah is the only God. This central concept, which is called **tawhid**, mirrors the monotheistic beliefs of the Jewish and Christian religions. Other parallels exist among the Islamic, Jewish, and Christian traditions. For example, figures and stories from the Old Testament and the Hebrew Bible recur in the Qur'an. The Judeo-Christian patriarch Abraham, for instance, is also a major figure for Muslims (who refer to him as Ibrahim). Islam, like Judaism and Christianity, emphasizes ethical behavior and charity. Islam also teaches that humans eventually will be judged, and that there is a heaven and hell. A key distinction between Islam and Christianity is that whereas Muslims believe Jesus was simply one in a line of 25 prophets, or teachers, throughout history and that Muhammad was the last and greatest of those prophets, Christians regard Jesus as the Son of God whose death redeemed sinful humanity.

By the time of Muhammad's death in 632, the formerly pagan Arabian Peninsula had come under the influence of Islam. In the years that followed, followers of Islam emerged from Arabia and aggressively spread their religion throughout the Middle East, parts of Asia, North Africa, and even Spain. They conquered towns and cities, built mosques (Islamic places of worship), and converted many thousands of people to Islam.

Today, Muslims constitute 99.8 percent of Turkey's population. About 8 in 10 are Sunnis, followers of Islam's main branch. The remainder of Turkey's Muslims belong to one of four Shiite sects, the largest of which is the Alevi Shia, a secretive group that historically suffered persecution.

Although nearly all of Turkey's

Two Turkish Muslims pray at the historic Blue Mosque, Istanbul. More than 99 percent of Turks are Muslims; the majority follow the Sunni branch of the faith, which is also the most common form of Islam among the more than 1 billion believers worldwide.

people are of the Muslim faith, Islam plays a less prominent role in the country's public life than it does in many Middle Eastern nations. After more than six centuries as part of the officially Islamic Ottoman Empire, independent Turkey became a secular state in 1928. The Turkish constitution mandates the separation of the state from any official religion. One of Atatürk's first acts as president was to distinguish Islamic law, or *Sharia*, from the laws of the Turkish government. By contrast, *Sharia* remains a basis of the legal systems of certain other Islamic nations. Among the few areas in the public sphere where the influence of the Muslim religion can still readily be seen is the Turkish flag, which consists of Islamic symbols: a star and crescent moon on a red field.

Among Turkey's extremely small non-Muslim population, Christianity claims the most adherents, with about 100,000. Given the fact that such a tiny fraction of Turks are Christians, it is interesting to note that the Greek Orthodox Church is based in Istanbul. About 25,000 Turks practice the Jewish faith. In the mid-20th century, almost 10 times as many Jews lived in Turkey. Most of them immigrated to the newly forged nation of Israel after 1948.

Despite the comparatively secular nature of Turkish society, non-Muslims have, at times, been the targets of radical Islamic terrorists—as when a bomb killed and injured many worshipers at a Jewish synagogue in Istanbul in the 1980s. Most Turkish Muslims decry such actions; some of them, in fact, rushed to the aid of the Jewish community in Istanbul and helped restore the damaged synagogue.

THE STRUCTURE OF TURKEY'S GOVERNMENT

Turkey has a form of government referred to as a republican parliamentary democracy. Much like the U.S. government, it has executive, legislative, and judicial branches of power. Unlike the United States—but like many other modern nations—Turkey divides executive power between a president and a prime minister. The president, Turkey's official head of state, is elected by parliament; a two-thirds majority is required. The term of office is seven years, and a president may not be reelected. The president officially appoints the country's prime minister (although for practical purposes, the prime minister is the leader of the political party controlling the largest number of seats in the single-chamber legislature, the Grand National Assembly). The president serves as commander-in-chief of the military, presides over the National Security Council, and appoints many types of government officials, including foreign ambassadors. Although lawmaking is in the hands of the assembly, the president may issue certain executive orders, may pardon criminals in special circumstances, and may ask the legislature to review any objectionable law before signing it into effect. If the lawmakers refuse to change the proposed law, the president may ask Turkey's Constitutional Court to overturn it. (The president appoints Constitutional Court members.)

Abdullah Gül served as provisional Prime Minister and foreign minister before becoming Turkey's 11th president in August 2007.

Turkey's president officially appoints each department head of the country's powerful Council of Ministers. However, council heads are proposed by the prime minister, who oversees the council. The Council of Ministers is similar to America's presidential cabinet. It oversees the ministries of the interior, foreign affairs, national defense, finance, industry and trade, agriculture and rural affairs, communication and transportation, health, education, labor, forestry, public works and resettlement, environment, energy and natural resources,

Kemal Atatürk, Turkey's revolutionary leader and first president, is still revered today. A statue or portrait of the national hero can be found in virtually every Turkish town. On November 10, the anniversary of his death, all activity in Turkey pauses for a two-minute period of solemn silence in Atatürk's memory.

tourism, and culture.

Turkey's parliament, or legislature, is the 550-member Grand National Assembly. Elections of assembly candidates are held every five years. This body exerts control over diverse areas of government. It can declare war and proclaim laws. It authorizes the printing of money, has the power to pardon convicted criminals, and approves the national budget. The assembly ratifies, or approves, international treaties and has overall authority over the Council of Ministers.

The judicial branch of government is responsible for administering the court system. Turkey actually has three court systems, each with a level of lower courts as well as higher courts of appeal. First, judicial courts form the largest component and handle most common cases, ranging from minor disputes between citizens to criminal prosecutions. These matters are decided by the presiding judge (or panel of judges), not by a jury. Decisions can be appealed. In America, the highest court of appeal is the U.S. Supreme Court. Turkey has divided its highest judicial court into two categories: The national Court of Appeals, or "Court of Cassation," reviews ordinary citizens' cases; the Constitutional Court decides whether disputed laws and government orders are in keeping with the Constitution.

A separate justice division deals only with matters involving military personnel. The third type of court, administrative, deals with legal issues involving government operations.

Since parliamentary elections affect who will appoint key government officials, political parties are alive and active in Turkey. Some have given themselves noble names; translated, they include the Virtue Party, the True Path Party, and the Motherland Party. Other parties include the Republican People's Party (the party of Kemal Atatürk) and the Democratic Left Party.

Turkey is divided into 81 government provinces. Each province has at least one representative in the Grand National Assembly; districts with greater populations have additional legislators. Each village throughout Turkey elects a "headman," or **muhtar**, every two years. The *muhtar* is the villagers' informal representative to the area's provincial government administration.

The voting age in Turkey is 18. Interestingly, men serving in the armed forces are not allowed to vote. All Turkish young men are required to serve in the military for 15 months. The armed forces—about half a million strong with almost a million more reserves—include an army, navy, and air force.

POWER AND POLITICS

Turkey's military played a dominant role in government and politics until the 1980s. Army officers launched coups and held power briefly in 1960 and 1980, and pressured the prime minister to resign in 1971. From the time of Kemal Atatürk, most of the country's presidents were career soldiers until Turgut Özal assumed office in 1989. Özal, like his successors Süleyman Demirel and Ahmet Necdet Sezer, came from a nonmilitary background.

Under Atatürk's regime, the Republican People's Party was the new Turkish nation's only political party. Atatürk was not only a remarkable reformer; he was Turkey's unchallenged leader for 15 years, until his death in November 1938. Since World War II, Turkey's leadership has been less stable and at times has been thrown into crises. Abrupt changes in government have continued into recent years, as the people have grappled with increasingly complex national issues.

The Democratic Left Party, organized in the late 1940s, quickly gained control of the Grand National Assembly. The new multiparty system did not lead to a more open democracy, however. To the contrary, during the 1950s, Turkey's political leaders repressed those who opposed them.

Military officers unhappy with the course the government was following took control in 1960. They demanded that a new national constitution be drafted. When this was done, the military returned the government to civilian leadership.

In 1982, after another period of military control, Turkey began what is known as its Third Republic. The constitution for the new government was passed in a national vote. It proclaimed Turkey to be a "democratic, secular and social state governed by the rule of law." By the 1990s, Muslim political activists were pushing for a more fundamentalist Islamic state. Opponents strongly insisted on a secular government. The question of Islamic influence in government remains a substantial political issue in Turkey. Indeed, a party with Islamic leanings, the Justice and Development Party, or AKP, won a stunning victory in 2002 elections, capturing 363 of the Grand National Assembly's 550 seats. Yet the party's leader, Recep Tayyip Erdogan, was barred from becoming prime minister because of a previous conviction for "inciting religious hatred." AKP officials, meanwhile, seemed careful to describe their party as moderate. No doubt they were concerned that the military—which has always assumed the role of guaranteeing the secular nature of the Turkish government—might be tempted to intervene. After another AKP victory in 2007, Erdogan controversially became prime minister. The main issue of the 2007 election was the role of Islam in Turkey's government.

The AKP's astonishing ascent to power capped a rather turbu-

Turkish women get ready to cast their votes in the November 2002 general election. Turkey's Islamic-based Justice and Development Party (AKP) won 34 percent of the vote, giving it a ruling majority in the country's parliament. Five years later, the AKP retained its majority.

lent decade of leadership changes in Turkey. In 1993 Tansu Çiller of the True Path Party became the nation's first female prime minister. Two years later, the Refah (Welfare) Party—noted for its firm Islamic support—became the majority party in the Turkish parliament. The Refah Party and the True Path Party formed a **coalition government**, and in 1996 Refah Party leader Necmettin Erbakan became the first prime minister in the history of the republic who was an Islamist (that is, a supporter of an increased role for Islam in society and government). His power was short-lived, however. The coalition lost its legislative majority in 1997. Erbakan was pressured by the military to resign, and the Refah Party was abolished by Turkey's Constitutional Court, following pressure by Turkey's armed forces and others concerned about Islamic influence in the Turkish government.

Mesut Yilmaz of the Motherland Party succeeded Erbakan—but was forced to exit after a very brief term because his administration lost a vote of confidence. Bülent Ecevit, who had served briefly as prime minister during the late 1970s, succeeded Yilmaz in 1999. But health problems and Turkey's two-year-long economic recession compelled Ecevit to call early elections for 2002, and the prime minister's Democratic Left Party failed to win a single assembly seat.

A Turkish girl wearing a traditional costume. About 80 percent of the country's people are ethnic Turks; the remaining 20 percent include Kurds, along with Greeks, Armenians, and others.

The People

The people of modern Turkey are known around the world for their generosity and hospitality. Even poor villagers treat visitors with incredible respect, serving them meals the villagers themselves cannot afford; the hosts believe God sent the guests to them, so every provision must be made to please their company. Rich or poor, Turks take pride in offering hospitality.

Approximately four-fifths of Turkey's people belong to the Turkish ethnic group—they are descendants of Seljuk and Ottoman Turks—and speak the Turkish language. Most of the remainder are Kurdish—but a few are of Greek, Armenian, or other descent. In all, more than 20 ethnic groups make up Turkey's population. Like other large countries, Turkey is a nation of diverse ethnic backgrounds and characteristics. Different localities are distinguished by such traits as the inhabitants' unique style of cooking, carpet weaving designs and coloring, and traditional dances.

Most Turks live in the western part of the country, near the Aegean coast and in the vicinity of Istanbul, Izmit, Bursa, and Izmir. Turkey is a country of more than 30,000 villages, but during the past 50 years increasing numbers of people have left behind the village life of their ancestors and moved to the cities and city suburbs. In 1900 the vast majority of Turks lived in small towns and rural areas; now the majority are moving or have moved to cities and suburbs. In the major cities, unskilled former villagers usually live in slums. Nevertheless, they can often find jobs that pay more money than they were earning in their hometowns. Moreover, they find that when they write home or return to their hometowns for a visit, they are typically treated with special respect by their families and old friends because they have "moved up in life."

Yet in many places in present-day Turkey, people still live much as they did during the centuries of the Ottomans. Turkey is a complex country: a land of the ancient, a land of the modern, a land of the ancient merging with the modern, and a land of the ancient steadfastly determined to cling to the old ways.

TURKISH LIFE

Life in modern Turkish cities is in many ways similar to life in other modern cities around the world. Old Istanbul is woefully overcrowded, and even more modern Ankara has growing shanty communities called ***gecekondus*** on its outskirts. Urban overcrowding has been exacerbated by the migration of large numbers of rural dwellers to towns and cities in the hopes of finding better jobs. It is estimated, for example, that more than a quarter million rural peasants move to Istanbul annually. Some of them find work as servants in the homes of the well-to-do.

In rural areas, many Turks live in small cottages made of stone or earthen bricks. Some have thatched roofs, like huts of old. If they

Turkey's population of more than 71 million is distributed fairly evenly throughout the country, as this map shows. Dense clusters of the population are located around Ankara, Istanbul, and Izmir, and along the coast of the Black Sea.

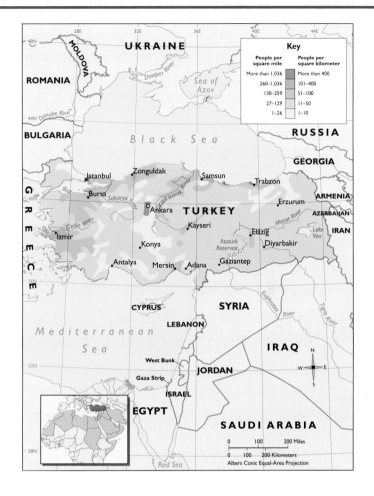

can afford it, villagers keep a modest guest room—not so much for traveling strangers as for regular gatherings of the village men. Frequent attendance at a home's guest room is, among other things, a display of respect to the owner of the home.

Turks place great value on the family. As in other Islamic countries, Turkish families regard the father as the head of the home and the primary provider. For many generations, women's main roles have been to bear children and manage the home.

Under the regime of Atatürk, Turkish women obtained a considerable measure of equality, compared with the women in most Islamic nations. For example, women were given the right to vote. Men were prohibited from taking more than one wife, as was customary previously. Even today in many Islamic countries, men can have up to four wives at one time, but women are not permitted to have more than one husband.

Since independence, more and more Turkish women have obtained an advanced education and have established careers. This trend is much more common in the cities of Turkey than in remote areas, where old customs are still very much alive. In fact, it is only in the cities that women are likely to be seen socializing with men in public.

Under Atatürk during the 1920s and 1930s, men and women of the new republic were encouraged to adopt Western dress. American clothes suddenly were in great demand, and enterprising merchants shipped large quantities of second-hand garments from New York for sale to the liberated Turks. Previously, Turks had dressed according to their status in society. For example, men who lived in cities wore different-colored fezzes, depending on their occupations.

Today, Western-style attire—from business suits and showy dresses to jeans and tennis shoes—is common. In 1988 the Turkish government took a remarkable action: it banned women attending universities from wearing scarves

The People of Turkey

Population: 71,892,808 (July 2008 est.)
Ethnic groups: Turkish, 80%; Kurdish, 20%
Religions: Muslim, 99.8%; other (mostly Christians and Jews), 0.2%
Age structure:
    0–14 years: 24.4%
    15–64 years: 68.6%
    65 years and over: 7%
Population growth rate: 1.013%
Birth rate: 16.15 births/1,000 population
Death rate: 6.02 deaths/1,000 population
Infant mortality rate: 36.98 deaths/ 1,000 live births
Life expectancy at birth:
    total population: 73.14 years
    males: 70.67 years
    females: 75.73 years
Total fertility rate: 1.87 children born/woman
Literacy (age 15 and over who can read and write): 87.4% (2004)

All figures are 2008 estimates unless otherwise indicated.
Source: CIA World Factbook, 2008.

Veiled Turkish women support the wearing of head scarves by female university students at a demonstration at Istanbul University. The head scarves, which are required by Islamic law, were banned at universities from 1988–2008 in accordance with the country's policy of separating the religious from the secular. Women have more freedoms in Turkey than in many other Muslim countries, including the right to gain educations, have careers, and participate in elections.

to class. This was a clear stand against certain long-standing Islamic customs and its 2008 repeal was controversial. As of this writing, the repeal has been suspended, and the ban continues. Some Turks, though, especially in rural areas, still wear traditional clothing. A traveler still might see men in old-style baggy trousers, while some women continue to veil their faces as did their great-great-grandmothers. Throughout the country, Turks often dress in ancestral attire on certain holidays and other special occasions.

Turkey has a young and growing population. Approximately half of its people are younger than 25. Muslim societies—including that of Turkey—treat older individuals with great respect. While many modern families in Western countries rely on elder-care systems to provide for aging parents and grandparents, Turkish families are more likely to care for older family members inside the home.

Similarly, public school students treat their teachers with special respect. They stand dutifully when a teacher enters a classroom. Teachers have a voice even in students' home life. For example, they may influence the children's television viewing habits.

A covered bazaar in Istanbul.

For centuries, the Turkish people have bought and sold wares at bazaars—the Middle Eastern counterpart to American shopping malls. Various shops and stalls in a bazaar sell almost every kind of item imaginable: spices, jewelry, bronze and copper pots and pans, handcrafts, carpets, clothing. Some bazaars are open-air, others enclosed. In most towns the bazaar is a center of activity.

Unlike items in most American stores, those in bazaar shops generally do not have take-it-or-leave-it price tags. The merchant expects to negotiate with customers—and customers learn to play the game shrewdly. Sellers (not unlike actors) initially might state an exorbitant price, then pretend to be hurt and insulted when a savvy customer offers only a fraction of the sum. Ultimately, they will agree on a price somewhere in between. Which of them has made the better deal? It is a regular, amusing competition that is part of the Turkish way of life.

TRANSPORTATION AND COMMUNICATION

Although travel to certain parts of rugged Turkey can be difficult if not grueling, Turkey's transportation infrastructure has been developed greatly over the last few decades. Turkey's communications systems and mass media also offer citizens a variety of options.

Bus travel is common throughout the country. Within many cities, buses form a vital part of mass transit systems; buses also transport people between rural towns and villages.

Train travel also is important. The government operates the Turkish train system, which consists of more than 6,000 miles (9,656 km) of railway. These rails transport people and cargo throughout the country and connect to Iran, Syria, and southern Europe. Meanwhile, major cities

Near Istanbul, ferryboats carry travelers across the Bosporus Strait. Turkey has a transportation system that is more modern than most of its neighbors in the Middle East.

use railways for mass transit. Ankara has a new rail network. Istanbul offers both underground and surface rail transportation.

Ferryboats carry travelers along and across the Bosporus Strait. To improve travel between the European and Asian sections of the country, however, two new bridges have been built across the strait in the past 30 years.

Armored personnel carriers belonging to the Turkish army guard the entrance to the town of Tunceli, in southeastern Turkey, in September 2002. The town was considered a stronghold of separatist Kurds until Turkey's military was sent there. Over the past century, relations between Turks and the country's Kurdish minority have been uneasy and often violent.

For long-distance and faster travel, Turkey has about 120 airports, most of them with paved runways. Those in major cities like Istanbul, Ankara, and Trabzon offer international flights.

Communications in Turkey are in many ways similar to communications in the United States and other Western countries. The nation has had a government-run broadcasting system, Turkish Radio and Television, for almost 40 years. During the 1990s private broadcasting operations developed rapidly. More than 1,000 radio stations, and more than 600 TV stations, now broadcast in Turkey. Most have only local ranges, but some can be received across large regions. There are some 35 national radio stations and about half that number of national television stations.

Turkey's telephone and Internet systems are expanding quickly. As of the year 2007, Turkey had 218,000 Internet service providers, with just over 12 million total users. Almost 19 million telephone lines and more than 52 million mobile phones were in use as of 2006. Satellites and undersea cables across the Mediterranean and Black Seas link Turkey's phone system with the international community.

Countless small newspapers and other periodicals are published throughout Turkey, as are more than 50 daily newspapers. Istanbul is the nation's publishing center. For the most part, the publishing industry enjoys freedom, although the government bans news reports that might foster disunity or undermine national security.

THE KURDS

In southeastern Turkey, in the mountainous region of the upper Euphrates and Tigris Rivers, lies the home of a unique group of people often in the news: the Kurds. In ancient times the Kurds were driven into the rugged highlands by conquering Armenians and Turks. For generations, they have been livestock farmers, migrating with the seasons to find grazing land for their animals and living in small villages. Theirs is a harsh terrain that supports only limited farming, with a bitter climate in which winter temperatures can drop below –50°F (–48°C).

Most Kurds are Sunni Muslims. Of the estimated 25–30 million Kurds in the Middle East, more than half are believed to live in Turkey, making up about 20 percent of the country's total population. Other Kurds live in the surrounding countries of Syria, Iraq, Iran, Azerbaijan, Armenia, and Georgia.

Kurds speak their own language, similar to ancient Persian, and they still write with the Arabic alphabet. Many Kurds also can converse in Turkish. In recent years, Kurds have become part of Turkish society outside their native areas. Like rural people elsewhere, some Kurds have moved to Turkey's urban districts. There they generally have been relegated to lowly jobs. Gradually, however, more young Kurds are obtaining an education and equipping themselves to improve their standing in society. Some, including former prime minister and president Turgut Özal, have risen to high positions.

In recent times, relations between Kurds and Turks have been strained if not overtly hostile. Many Kurds have come to regard the Turkish military as brutal oppressors and the government as virtually a foreign regime that ignores their welfare. They feel shut out of Turkish society—and in significant ways, they have been isolated, not only because of where they live but because of their culture and heritage. Many Turks, for their part, have viewed the Kurds as wild, tribal mountaineers who live by their own laws and are not above marauding outlying villages and farms, particularly during hard times.

Kurds did launch a rebellion soon after Turkey became an independent republic in the 1920s. Atatürk responded with force. Further revolts occurred in the coming decades, as Kurds resisted Atatürk's policies of modernization and secular government. They also opposed the changes he made in the country's alphabet and language. By the 1970s, some Kurdish leaders were pushing for an independent nation of Kurds. The Turkish military quashed the movement.

Some of Turkey's government leaders refused to recognize the existence of the Kurdish minority even into modern times. Ultimately, however, the government acknowledged a distinct Kurdish culture with unique customs, interests, and needs and authorized separate Kurdish schools.

But the tension continues. The Kurdistan Workers' Party (PKK), organized in the late 1970s by a Marxist (communist) revolutionary named Abdullah Öcalan, began building a formidable guerrilla force to take on the Turkish military. His organization found eager volunteers among the Kurds, along with weapons, money, and training from Turkey's hostile southern neighbor, Syria, and other countries. While the PKK's ultimate socialist objectives were at times a little difficult to discern, its call for an independent Kurdish homeland was clear.

In 1984 Öcalan's guerrillas began attacks on Turkish military posts along the Syrian border. By the following decade, the PKK had escalated the violence with acts of urban terrorism. PKK units destroyed and damaged factories, power and phone lines, and other public utility equipment and facilities. They kidnapped foreign tourists and carried out a series of bombings on tourist sites and public places, apparently with the intention of disrupting Turkey's important tourism industry, which receives as many as 8 million visitors annually. Their targets came to include not only Turks, but Kurds whom the PKK accused of pro-Turkish leanings.

For its part, the Turkish government's efforts to suppress the PKK were every bit as ruthless as the tactics of Öcalan's group. In the 1990s soldiers sent into the Kurdish region burned villages believed to be sympathetic to the PKK and slaughtered the villagers' cattle. Police and security agencies, meanwhile, arrested and tortured suspected PKK supporters in efforts to obtain information.

Some foreign nations sternly criticized Turkey for its Kurdish policy. Many Turks, on the other hand, insisted that their government had little alternative. Stephen Kinzer summed up the merciless nature of the struggle in his book *Crescent & Star: Turkey Between Two Worlds*. "The brutality of [the government's] tactics," Kinzer wrote, "is indisputable, as is the brutality of the PKK's rebellion." By the end of the 20th century, the conflict had claimed the lives of more than 30,000 people—guerrillas, soldiers, and civilians alike. In addition, the fighting had displaced many Kurds from their homes and villages.

However, by the late 1990s the Turkish government had gotten the upper hand. After being forced to evacuate his longtime base in northern Syria in 1999, Öcalan was captured in Kenya by Turkish agents and flown back to Turkey. At his trial, he called on the PKK to abandon its armed struggle but was nevertheless sentenced to death. In January 2000 the PKK did formally announce an end to its use of violence, declaring its intention to work within the political system to help Turkey's Kurds. But in 2007, more fighting broke out between Turkish soldiers and the PKK.

THE ARMENIANS AND YÜRÜKS

Another historically important—and tragic—group in Turkey and neighboring countries are the Armenians. They descend from an ancient people who settled in what is today the Republic of Armenia and eastern Turkey around the seventh century B.C. The kingdom of Greater Armenia was established in eastern Anatolia by a general named Artaxias during the second century B.C. His great-grandson Tigranes substantially enlarged the kingdom. The region became a province of the Roman Empire in 55 B.C., and in the fourth century A.D. it embraced Christianity as its official religion.

Later, Armenians were mistreated and taxed heavily by the

Byzantine leaders. This was because of differences in their Christian beliefs and because of the Byzantines' fear that Armenians might develop friendships with neighboring Persia—a dangerous enemy of the empire. Yet, over the centuries, industrious Armenians prospered as craft makers, merchants, and even political leaders.

The Armenians developed their own alphabet and established a unique culture that was preserved over the centuries. When Arabs and Turks began invading the Anatolian Peninsula, Armenia

Boatloads of Armenian men, women, and children seek refuge on a French warship off the coast of Syria, October 1915. Hundreds of thousands of Armenians living in the Ottoman Empire died at the hands of the Turks during World War I.

managed to survive during the early centuries. It finally was subdued in 1375 by the Mamelukes. In the early 1500s, the territory became part of the Ottoman Empire.

During the next four centuries, western Armenia was under the Ottoman thumb. Eastern Armenia, meanwhile, passed first into Persian, then Russian, control. Within the Ottoman Empire, Armenians, Greeks, Jews, and other non-Muslims (known as **millets**) were allowed a degree of self-rule. The Ottomans let them keep their church systems, laws, and customs.

In the 19th and 20th centuries, Armenians were persecuted by the Muslim majority and oppressed by the government. During the 1890s and again 20 years later during World War I, the Ottoman regime, together with Kurdish forces, killed staggering numbers of Armenians, accusing them of disloyalty.

The Ottoman government feared that Russia was poised to seize control of the region, uniting Russian Armenians with their distant relatives in eastern Turkey. Russia and the Ottoman Empire were foes during World War I, and the Armenian territory between them was a war zone. If Ottoman Armenians joined the side of Russia, it would pose a crisis in the Ottomans' war effort. (In fact, Russia did take control of the eastern Armenian region two years after the war ended.)

In 1915 the Ottoman authorities told Armenians it was going to relocate them. After they left their homes, the Armenians were led on forced marches, some of which ended in deserts inside present-day Syria, where the Armenians were left to die of starvation, dehydration, or exposure. Other groups were simply massacred by soldiers. According to Armenian sources, up to 1.5 million Armenians perished during this time. Some survivors made their way to Russian territory. Among the small number of ethnic Armenians in Turkey today, a sizeable proportion lives in Istanbul.

Tension still exists between ethnic Armenians and the rest of Turkey. In 2007, a Turkish nationalist assassinated a Turkish-American journalist who had written about the forced marches. Turkish citizens of all ethnicities—as well as the federal government—condemned the murder, but many Armenians worried that it was not an isolated incident.

The Yürük people, who inhabit the Taurus Mountains in southern Turkey, are another small but fascinating minority. Even in modern times, hundreds of thousands of Turks—possibly as many as a million—continue the shepherding life of their forebears, herding sheep and goats. More than half of these modern nomads are Yürüks. Some observers consider them "pure Turks," little changed from their Asian ancestors of many centuries past. Their language is a quaintly old variation of Turkish. They live off their herds, making meat and goat cheese staples of their diet and sleeping in goat-hair tents. In these ways, they are indeed much like the Turks who originally settled Anatolia.

A view of Ankara at night. The city, located in the central Anatolian highlands, has been the capital of the country since 1923. Today, more than 3.7 million people live in Ankara.

Communities

Turkey is a country where things that are very old exist alongside things that are decidedly modern. In places, centuries-old structures are flanked or surrounded by new buildings. Both European and Arabic influences can be seen not just in the architecture but throughout Turkish culture.

ANKARA

Ankara, with an estimated 2007 population of 3.76 million, has been Turkey's capital since independence. Most government offices and major businesses are headquartered there. Situated on the central Anatolian plateau, it is an old city that originated long before the Ottoman Empire began. Compared with Istanbul, however, Ankara is strikingly modern, its skyline marked by high-rises.

The capital has grown rapidly in recent decades. One notably unpleasant feature is the city's wintertime pall of

The Blue Mosque, which appears in front of the Hagia Sophia in this photograph, is one of the famous landmarks of Istanbul. The mosque, completed in 1616, is a classic example of Ottoman architecture. Istanbul is Turkey's largest city and major cultural center; its glorious history dates back thousands of years.

smog, caused by the burning of coal to heat residences and workplaces. Another unhappy sight are Ankara's shantytowns, where tens of thousands of residents live in squalor. Many moved to the capital from rural areas, in search of jobs and improved living conditions, but have found little but poverty.

ISTANBUL

One of the world's most ancient and famous cities, Istanbul is situated primarily on the European continent at the western side of the Bosporus Strait. Formerly named Constantinople and, before that, Byzantium, it is today Turkey's largest city by far, with an estimated 2007 population of more than 10.7 million. The city served as the capital of the Eastern Roman Empire from the 4th to the 15th centuries, then became the capital of the Ottoman Empire. Historians believe one reason Ankara, not Istanbul, was chosen as capital of the Turkish Republic was to establish a symbolic break from the many centuries of Byzantine and Ottoman **imperialism** and to define the new Turkey as a wholly independent country.

Although no longer a capital, Istanbul remains Turkey's cultural and business center because of its size, location, and legacy. To many outsiders, Istanbul is the city that first comes to mind when they think of Turkey. Because of its crucial location at the juncture of Asia and Europe, Istanbul is a true "melting pot" of diverse peoples and cultures. It is also one of the most fascinating tourist destinations in the world, with ancient palaces, ruins, Byzantine churches, mosques, and other interesting structures that span the city's long history as a world power center.

Many of the most popular sites are in the old, central part of the city, called Stamboul. Not far away are modern homes, hotels, parks, and industrial developments. Bridges across the Bosporus carry both quiet foot traffic and noisy cars and buses, demonstrating that Istanbul is a city of the present as well as the past.

OTHER CITIES

Izmir, Turkey's third-largest city, claimed about 2.6 million residents by 2007. Located on the west coast, it is a major Aegean seaport and one of Turkey's leading manufacturing centers. Other large cities in Turkey include Bursa, Adana, and the port of Iskenderun.

In the European region of Thrace, Edirne lies near the border with Greece. This once was the Roman city of Adrianople; later, it was of major strategic importance to the Ottoman Empire.

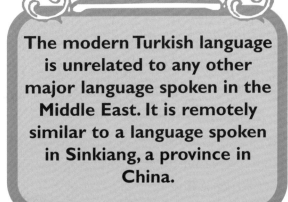

The modern Turkish language is unrelated to any other major language spoken in the Middle East. It is remotely similar to a language spoken in Sinkiang, a province in China.

HOLIDAYS AND OBSERVANCES

Like people in countries around the world, Turks celebrate a variety of civic and religious holidays. In the former category, two important observances in Turkey occur on April 23: National Independence Day and Children's Day. National Independence Day commemorates the formation of the Grand National Assembly, Turkey's legislature, in 1923. Children's Day, initiated by Atatürk, recognizes young people, whom he considered to be among Turkey's greatest assets. This kind of holiday is rare among the world's nations. On Children's Day, Turkey's families are expected to dress their children in new outfits. Some Turkish communities consider it the town's responsibility to ensure that even poor children with little means receive new clothes for Children's Day.

A solemn observance in Turkey is the anniversary of Atatürk's death, November 10. The revered president died at 9:05 in the morning, and at that time on each anniversary, citizens unite in two minutes of silent remembrance.

As a Muslim nation, Turkey observes Islamic holidays. The Islamic month of Ramadan is a period of fasting during the daylight hours; devout Muslims refrain even from drinking water. After sunset each day, worshipers break the fast with a hardy supper. Ramadan ends with a three-day festival called Eid al-Fitr. This is a time of goodwill, when people visit one another and renew old friendships, and women prepare sweets for neighborhood children.

Another Islamic holiday, Eid al-Adha, is a day of sacrifice. It remembers the story, told in the Qur'an, of the patriarch Ibrahim's willingness to sacrifice his son Ismail as ordered by Allah. (A variation of the story also appears in the Bible.) At the last instant Allah provides a ram for slaughter instead. Many Turkish families accordingly butcher a sheep on this day, symbolizing the ancient sacrifice.

Some of the regional festivals in Turkey aren't intended to commemorate any patriotic or religious event, but are simply to be enjoyed. Istanbul is the scene of the monthlong International Arts Festival, while Troy is host to the Drama Festival. One unusual affair, held in the village of Selçuk, is an annual camel festival. Camels engage in shoving antics and a "beauty" competition while the humans in attendance enjoy music, food, and dancing.

SPORTS AND RECREATION

As president, Atatürk encouraged physical fitness. May 19, his birthday, now is a national holiday called Youth and Sports Day. Turks take sports and physical exercise quite seriously. At one time, the republic's General Directorate of Youth and Sports was a cabinet office of the government.

Soccer is the favorite sport in Turkey. Pickup games in streets and open lots are common sights in Turkish towns and cities. Three professional leagues showcase the talents of the best players. Istanbul has several of the leading professional teams.

Wrestling has long been a popular sport in the region of modern-day Turkey; in the *Iliad* Homer describes a wrestling match that was held as part of a funeral festival. A popular form of the sport unique to Turkey is called Kirkpinar wrestling. Today, an annual Kirkpinar wrestling tournament is held in Edirne.

Turkish soccer teams have not been particularly strong in Olympic competition during the past half century. The country's world-class weightlifters and wrestlers, however, have claimed a number of Olympic medals. One sport unique to eastern Turkey is called *cirit*, in which horseback riders compete to catch javelins hurled in the air as they ride past.

Other organized sports in Turkey include volleyball and basketball. Athletes also compete in a form of "greased wrestling," in which the opponents oil their bodies to make them almost impossible to lock into a hold. Popular outdoor pastimes among Turks include mountain hiking and, in a few areas, snow skiing.

For recreation, Turkish children can amuse themselves with common diversions such as sticks, jump ropes, rocks, chalk, or crayons. Some who live in the larger towns and cities have access to sliding boards and other playground equipment, just like American youngsters. They also enjoy movies, video games, and television—pastimes not available in remote villages. Especially popular with Turkish children are colorful puppet shows.

Families often picnic or find lakes, pools, or beaches at which to swim. They like to stroll through town and visit friends.

FOOD AND DRINK

The natural Turkish diet is healthful and varied, using the country's wonderful assortment of food products. It has been this way for thousands of years. We know that in the ancient Hittite Kingdom, for example, people made bread, grew vegetables and fruits, and raised livestock for milk and cheese. (Meat and fish were reserved for Hittite nobility.) Today, the Turkish diet is likewise balanced and made interesting by the culinary style of the Anatolian region.

Eastern Mediterranean cooking turns often to vegetables, including zucchinis, eggplants, pepper plants, and tomatoes.

Baklava, a sweet, flaky pastry, is a popular dessert in Turkey.

Roasted lamb and mutton are favorite meats and are almost always served with rice. Rice wrapped in grape or cabbage leaves and cooked is called *dolmas*. Turks are especially noted for their grilled shish kebab, a skewered arrangement of meat, tomato, green pepper, and onion. Lentil and other vegetable soups are popular. Goat milk provides yogurt and cheese. Olives are common table items. The smell of fresh-baked bread arouses hearty appetites. Garlic seasoning is popular. And since the nation is flanked on three sides by the sea, Turks living in coastal regions naturally take advantage of the abundant seafood.

In their desserts, Turks often use fruits as well as natural sugar. One of Turkey's most famous desserts is baklava, a rich, layered pastry saturated with honey and laced with chopped nuts.

Tea is Turkey's most popular drink. Turks drink it not only at home and at restaurants, but also at work. Many Turks drink tea throughout the day. In 1986 Turks faced a significant crisis when the nuclear reactor disaster at Chernobyl, a town in the Ukraine to the north, spread radioactivity across the Black Sea region. Turkish tea, found to contain dangerous levels of radioactivity, temporarily could not be bought, much to the dismay of millions of regular drinkers.

COLORFUL ARTS AND CRAFTS

Of all the items that might be found at a Turkish bazaar, the country is most famous worldwide for its carpets, which feature colorful geometric and pictorial patterns. The Italian traveler and chronicler Marco Polo commented on the fantastic color and beauty of Seljuk carpets when he passed through the region in the 1200s. Turkish weavers make these true works of art in different sizes. Today, many tourists and foreign importers buy them as luxury items, largely for the carpets' ornate value. Originally, however, they served practical purposes. The Seljuks wove carpets of sheep's wool to cover the bare floors and clay walls of their huts; this helped keep the interior dry and warm. The heavy fabrics also made useful blankets on cold nights.

A selection of Turkish handicrafts made by bronzesmiths and silversmiths.

Each Seljuk tribe was known for its carpets' unique design pattern, and skill at carpet weaving became a matter of great pride. Over time, the rugs were considered items of real value. Small girls began learn-

An abundance of beautiful Roman mosaics such as the one pictured here have been uncovered in the Turkish town of Antakya (called Antioch in Roman times).

ing to weave from their mothers, and when they married, carpets were part of their **dowry**.

Today, some girls learn weaving in school. Others learn from their elders. Besides the typical flat-woven rugs (called *kilim*), Turkish carpets may be of the knotted type. Some weavers make elaborate products of silk. As in other Muslim countries, a special type of carpet is the small prayer rug, which is decorated with Islamic symbols.

Another type of Turkish craft originally developed for practical use and now prized by foreign collectors for its display value is decorative kitchenware. Potters, coppersmiths, and bronze artisans produce ornate plates, pots, and bowls. It's an ancient craft. Different varieties of objects are common to specific regions. Iznik, for example, became famous many centuries ago for its bluish glazed earthenware. Kütahya, a city in western Turkey, is especially noted for its pottery with elegant pictorial designs. Much of the metalwork and pottery that comes out of Turkey today is mass-produced in factories, but traditional artisans continue to handcraft beautiful products just as their ancestors did.

Turkish crafters and artists also produce fine stained glass, miniatures, jewelry, and artistic mirrors. A curious form of artistry particular to Turkey is the carving of smoking pipes from a clay-like mineral called meerschaum. Meerschaum pipes are lightweight and are treasured by pipe smokers the world over because with age, they gradually turn from pure white to rustic brown. Turkish pipe makers carve meerschaum into a variety of beautiful shapes.

The pictorial arts blossomed during Atatürk's presidency. In traditional Islamic society, the portrayal of people and other living subjects in art is forbidden. The Ottomans followed this teaching, declaring that to paint or carve a human was a kind of idolatry, but Atatürk permitted artists and artisans to open up the scope of their work. As a result, Turkish art is particularly rich among the art of Muslim nations.

Turkey is noted especially for its miniature paintings. This style of art is ages old, harking back to the years when gifted but starving artists scrambling for food money would produce sketches "on the fly" for customers at city bazaars or street stalls. The detail they provided—and continue to provide—presents a pictorial record of life in Turkey, present and past.

MUSIC AND DANCE

The music and other performing arts of Turkey are enthralling. Some Turkish music is for ceremonies and dancing, some for religious observances, some for military accompaniment and fanfare, and some for storytelling. Certain forms originated many centuries ago, before the Byzantine Empire. Over time, outside influences were incorporated into Turkish music. These influences have included European symphonic music and, today, American pop and rock sounds. Apart from the language in which songs are sung, Turkish pop recordings sound much like those produced in the United States.

Turkish folk music employs wood and metal flutes; drums, bells, and other percussion instruments; and plucked instruments. A common stringed instrument is the Turkish *saz*. A thin-necked, usually gut-strung instrument with a bowl-shaped body, it is made in different lengths.

Whirling dervishes perform in Konya. The dervishes follow a mystical branch of Islam known as Sufism that emerged in the 13th century. The Sufis perform their dance, the *Sema*, one week a year in commemoration of the death of Sufism's founder, Mevlana Jelaleddin Rumi.

Traditional dance forms are among the many customs Turkey's various ethnic groups have maintained.

Traditional music also accompanies ancient and sometimes exotic dances. Dance styles common to specific regions of the country have been handed down from generation to generation. The dancers often dress in colorful handmade costumes. Some dance forms, such as sword dancing, are breathtaking.

The dance of the mysterious whirling dervishes dates to the Seljuk era in Anatolia. Sufis—members of an Islamic mystical sect—the whirling dervishes performed their dance in order to put themselves into a trancelike state during which, they believed, they approached oneness with Allah. President Atatürk, as part of his mission to modernize Turkey during the 1920s and 1930s, banned the ancient dance form. But today, the year-end Rites of the Whirling Dervishes in Konya continues the fantastic tradition.

Music also is used to accompany ballads. Storytelling—whether musical, poetic, or narrative—has always been an important part of Turkish culture. Some of the ancient ballads recall Seljuk legends. A long-popular storytelling character is the comical yet wise "Hoça" from the town of Aksehir. Like Mother Goose tales in America, Hoça tales are well known to Turkish children.

A Turkish man holds his country's flag during a demonstration in Solingen, Germany. Because of Turkey's location between Europe, Russia, and the Middle East, the country has had a key role in world affairs.

Foreign Relations

Unavoidably, Turkey's geographic location has determined the underlying nature of its relations with foreign countries. An overview by Turkey's Ministry of Foreign Affairs points out that the republic has "European, Balkan, Mediterranean, Middle Eastern, Caucasian and Asian identities all at the same time. [This] has exerted a strong influence on [Turkey's] foreign policy choices and has necessitated a multidimensional foreign policy. In this context, the primary objectives of Turkish foreign policy are to establish and to develop friendly relations with all countries, in particular with neighboring ones; to promote and to take part in regional and international cooperation; to resolve disputes through peaceful means and to contribute to regional peace, stability, security and prosperity."

Since independence Turkey has for the most part managed to avoid the recurring conflicts that have engulfed the

Middle East—though that is not to say Turkey's foreign relations have been free of tensions. Turkey's relative neutrality can be attributed in part to the diplomatic skills of its first president, Mustafa Kemal Atatürk. Atatürk deftly avoided alliances and policies that might draw his country into international conflict. Even today, Turkey's national motto—coined by Atatürk—is "Peace at home, peace in the world."

As the clouds of World War II gathered during the 1930s, Turkey pursued alliances intended to secure its eastern and western borders. In the east, it signed the Saadabad Pact with Iran, Iraq, and Afghanistan. In the west, it joined the Balkan Entente with Greece, Yugoslavia, and Romania. Turkey managed to stay out of the Second World War altogether until the final months. In 1945, after the war, Turkey became a founding member of the United Nations.

TURKEY AND GREECE: UNHAPPY NEIGHBORS

However, Turkey's relations with other countries have been uneasy and at times tragic. Warfare with Greece, its western neighbor, was part of Atatürk's fight for independence after World War I. After the invading Greek army was driven from the Anatolian Peninsula, part of the peace accord entailed one of history's most massive population shifts. Christians living in Thrace migrated to Greece, while Greek Muslims relocated to Turkey. Some 2 million to 3 million individuals crossed the border between the two countries.

That episode was just one example of Turkey's periodically stormy relations with Greece. One especially sensitive point of contention, which has led to international political complications, has been Cyprus, a Mediterranean island some 50 miles (80 km) off Turkey's southern coast. Once a British colony, Cyprus became an independent republic in 1960. Most Cypriots are of Greek lineage, but over the centuries a growing Turkish population settled there.

Greeks and Turks have not lived in harmony on the mountainous

A United Nations soldier patrols the "Green Line," which divides the island of Cyprus into Greek and Turkish sections. Control of Cyprus has been a thorny issue between the two countries for many years; since the 1970s the UN has maintained the Green Line buffer zone.

island. The Turkish government threatened to intervene in island affairs in 1964, charging that the Greek majority repressed Turkish Cypriots. But Turkey was warned off by the United States, which wanted to keep peace between Greece and Turkey—both of which were important U.S. allies in the region and members of the North Atlantic Treaty Organization (NATO), a U.S.-led alliance designed to counteract the threat presented by the Soviet Union and its Eastern European satellite nations. Ten years later, Greek Cypriots in the island's military took over the government. Fearing that the new leaders would let Greece **annex** the island, Turkey this time sent an armed force to occupy the northern part of Cyprus.

Again, the U.S. government opposed the Turks' use of force. The American Congress voted to halt U.S. military aid to Turkey; Turkey, in response, shut down American bases. The standoff lasted four years until Turkey and the United States renewed their military agreements. Cyprus later was divided, with Greeks controlling the larger southern section and Turks governing the north.

During the 1990s, the governments of Turkey and Greece began discussions and signed a number of agreements intended to foster greater cooperation in the region. But Ankara remains wary of

Athens. Turkish-Greek disputes during the late 20th century included disagreements over undersea oil drilling in the Aegean Sea.

RELATIONS WITH THE RUSSIANS

Turkey has had a complicated, largely antagonistic relationship with the countries of the former Soviet Union to the north. In Ottoman times, the Turks were the aggressors, spreading their influence northward around the Black Sea by the 17th century. As the Ottoman Empire deteriorated, Russia pushed back the Ottoman borders to the northern Black Sea coast and down into the Caucasus region along the eastern shore. For many years—into the mid-1900s—Russia also sought at least partial control of the Turkish straits and the Sea of Marmara, the key to naval and trade access between the Black Sea and the Mediterranean.

The first series of Russo-Turkish wars, from 1676 to 1739, mainly were attempts by Russia to establish ports on the Black Sea and to drive the Ottomans out of the Balkan states. Later hostilities throughout the 18th and 19th centuries involved those and other international issues farther afield. Slowly but relentlessly, the Russians and southern European countries gained ground against the Ottomans. By the end of the Balkan Wars of 1912–13 against Montenegro, Bulgaria, Greece, Serbia, and Romania, the Ottoman Empire had lost most of its European territory.

World War I dramatically affected the Black Sea region and its politics. As the Ottoman Empire crumbled, the Russian Revolution brought the countries across the Black Sea into a communist union. Atatürk accepted help from Soviet communists in his war of liberation after World War I. He was wary of communism, however, and considered the Soviets a threat to his new nation's self-rule. His fears were borne out after his death, when Soviet dictator Joseph Stalin in the late 1940s demanded that Turkey share control of the straits. Turkey, backed by the United States and other anticommunist governments, stood firm.

During the Korean War (1950–53), Turkey contributed soldiers to the United Nations force that helped defend South Korea against Soviet- and Chinese-backed communist North Korea. In 1952 Turkey also became a member of NATO, a U.S.-led alliance, organized in 1949, that included Western European nations and Canada and whose primary mission was to counter the Soviet Union's communist expansion across Eastern Europe after World War II. As part of its involvement, the Ankara government allowed the United States to set up military bases in Turkish territory.

But after Stalin's death in 1953, the Soviet Union made friendly overtures toward the Ankara government. Besides abandoning past claims to disputed lands between the countries, the Soviets gave Turkey substantial industrial aid. These actions were designed to undermine Turkish-American relations.

Tension between the world superpowers during the latter part of the 20th century sometimes involved Turkey. One of the most dangerous situations, which occurred in autumn 1962, is known to history as the Cuban Missile Crisis.

President John F. Kennedy signs Proclamation 3504, authorizing a U.S. Navy quarantine of Cuba, on October 23, 1962. The blockade was intended to keep Soviet ships carrying military supplies from reaching the island. The 13-day Cuban Missile Crisis in October 1962 was resolved when the Soviet Union agreed to remove its nuclear missiles from Cuba. In return, the United States withdrew its own nuclear missiles from Turkey.

This was at the height of the cold war, a generation of fear and distrust between the United States and the Soviet Union. The crisis arose after the Soviet Union began building nuclear missile bases in Cuba, its communist ally in the Caribbean Sea less than 100 miles (161 km) from the tip of Florida. U.S. president John F. Kennedy demanded that the missiles be removed. Kennedy ordered the United States Navy to blockade Cuba, preventing the arrival of more nuclear warheads. The president considered invading the island in order to destroy the missiles. If America had carried out such an invasion, many scholars now believe, it would have ignited a cata-strophic nuclear war between the superpowers—a scenario that also seemed likely at the time.

After a week of almost unbearable tension on both sides of the Atlantic, the crisis was resolved when Soviet premier Nikita S. Khrushchev agreed to remove the missiles from Cuba. In return, President Kennedy agreed to remove nuclear missiles that had been established at U.S. military sites in Turkey.

With the breakup of the Soviet Union in 1991, the cold war effec-tively ended. In place of the former communist superpower, more than a dozen independent countries—the largest of which is Russia—emerged. In the post-Soviet era, Turkey has expressed optimism for building positive relations with the now-independent states around the Black Sea.

RELATIONS WITH ISRAEL AND THE WEST

Turkey's membership in NATO and its other pro-Western policies have set it apart politically from the mainstream Islamic world. Other issues have created tension between the Turkish republic and its Arab neighbors. For example, bad feelings have existed historically between Turkey and Syria to the south. One source of animosity is the disputed Hatay district on their Mediterranean border. After World War I, Hatay became part of Syria, a French territory, despite the residence there of many Turkish people. In 1938, after almost 20 years of unrest, the League of Nations conducted a popular vote to decide the fate of Hatay. Most citizens voted to become part of Turkey, and the following year France allowed Turkey to annex the area. This enraged many Syrians.

Another divisive issue between Turkey and Syria, and between Turkey and the Arab countries generally, is Turkey's relationship with Israel. Most of the Arab world has considered Jewish Israel the archenemy. Turkey, however, formally recognized Israel when the latter nation established itself in 1948. Israel is basically pro-Western, as is Turkey. While people of the two countries have fundamental differences, Turkey refrained from joining Syria and other Arab Muslim countries in their series of conflicts against Israel during the second half of the 20th century.

In fact, the government administrations in Ankara and Tel Aviv progressively have moved to strengthen ties. A "strategic alignment" culminating in 1996 and the Turkey-Israel Free Trade Agreement the following year served as notable recent signs of Turkish-Israeli amity. The countries have established economic, political, academic, cultural, and even military interaction. For example, trade between the countries has increased markedly and cooperative industrial projects have been launched. Turkey recently agreed to sell and transport freshwater to Israel from the Manavgat River. Performing artists have frequently exchanged cultural visits. And the Turkish military has sought Israeli military intelligence and technological aid in countering opposition forces.

Turkish-Israeli friendliness has angered Muslims across the Arab world and inside Turkey itself. On occasion protestors have taken to the streets. Many Turks openly sympathized with Palestinian victims during 2002 Arab-Israeli hostilities in the West Bank and Gaza areas.

However, Turkey's government seems to have successfully

threaded a course through the maze of complex and treacherous issues involving Muslim-Western relations. One commentator has observed that despite their animosity, none of the Arab governments severed relations with Turkey when the latter extended diplomatic recognition to Israel in 1948.

In the aftermath of the September 11, 2001, terrorist attack on the United States, Turkey strongly denounced the assault. During the next year, it contributed some 1,400 military personnel to a multinational force sent to Afghanistan to demolish the terrorist network believed responsible for the attack. Itself a target of Kurdish terrorism, the Ankara government was particularly sympathetic to the United States. In a statement on terrorism, Turkey's foreign ministry proclaimed: "Terrorism violates fundamental human rights, particularly the right to live, and can have no justification under any circumstances. It is an evil that strikes at the very core of democracy, civil society as well as economic and social development. . . . Turkey is of the opinion that terrorism cannot be

The defense ministers of NATO nations at a 2000 meeting in England. Since joining NATO in 1952, Turkey has been an important member of the organization because of its strategic location.

associated with any religion, culture, geography or ethnic group. Terrorist organizations exist everywhere in the world; therefore, the fight against terrorism is the common fight of the civilized world."

BORDER ISSUES

A variety of regional issues have complicated Turkey's relations with neighboring countries. Over the last century, for example, Turkey has harnessed its rivers to irrigate nearby land for farmers and to provide hydroelectric power. Its plans for such projects on the Euphrates and Tigris Rivers have concerned the governments of Syria and Iraq, Turkey's neighbors downriver, because activities in Turkey could affect usage of the rivers in those countries.

The existence of significant numbers of Kurdish people in eastern Turkey as well as several neighboring countries—along with the Kurdish dream of an independent Kurdistan—has also complicated Turkey's relations with its neighbors. In the wake of the Gulf War in 1991, for example, the Iraqi government brutally suppressed a Kurdish uprising in its north, sending tens of thousands of Iraqi Kurds fleeing across the border into Turkey. The government in Ankara did not welcome the refugees, fearing they might incite Turkish Kurds to revolt. (This was, after all, at a time when the PKK was carrying on a campaign of terrorism to win a Kurdish homeland within Turkey.) Only reluctantly and under international pressure did Turkish officials allow the Iraqi Kurds to settle.

By 2003 the prospect of another Persian Gulf war threatened to further complicate the already delicate Kurdish question. Amid accusations that Iraq had failed to comply with obligations to dismantle its programs for the development of so-called weapons of mass destruction, the U.S. administration of President George W. Bush contemplated an invasion to topple the regime of the Iraqi dictator, Saddam Hussein. Many observers wondered whether the Kurds in northern Iraq—who, under the protection of U.S. and British military

Kurdish refugees fight for space on passing trucks in Bakhtaran, Iraq, April 1991. After the end of the Persian Gulf War, hundreds of thousands of Kurds fled Iraq for the relative safety of Turkey and Iran.

forces, had basically enjoyed autonomy since the early 1990s—would try to use the occasion to establish an independent Kurdish state. Turkey strongly opposed such a development, as Turkish Kurds might be encouraged to unite with their ethnic cousins across the border.

POLISHING THE INTERNATIONAL IMAGE

Besides making it a land of political importance and a special attraction to foreign tourists, Turkey's location has given it a dark distinction, especially in the past half-century. Drug rings dealing in heroin, opium, and other substances are based in Istanbul. From there, they control the passage of illegal narcotics between Europe and Asia.

Another concern brought about by its location is shipping pollution. The Turkish straits have been used ever more heavily in the last century by vessels calling at Istanbul and moving between the Black Sea and the Aegean and Mediterranean. Water pollution and the threat of oil spills in or near the Bosporus and Dardanelles and the Sea of Marmara worry residents on both sides of the straits. A major spill could affect not only the Turkish shorelines but also the waters and coasts of other Black Sea and Aegean islands and countries.

More than 3 million Turkish nationals work in foreign countries. More than half of them have jobs in Germany, and a growing number are taking positions in the countries of the former Soviet Union.

For some time, Turkey has sought membership in the increasingly influential European Union (EU), which Turkish officials view as key to improving their nation's economic prospects. In fact, Turkey's Justice and Development Party made EU admission its top foreign policy priority. The EU initially rejected Turkey's membership bid but agreed in December 2002 to review the matter in two years, pending the implementation of reforms by Turkey. Of significant concern to the EU was Turkey's human rights record. Some progress has been made—such as the lifting, in 2002, of the 15-year state of emergency in the Kurdish southeast, where the brutality of Turkish security forces was well documented. But, according to a report released in January 2003 by the Paris-based International Federation of Human Rights Leagues, torture remains a frequently used tool of the Turkish police and military. Victims, the report said, include criminal as well as political suspects, including Kurds.

There is no doubt that Turkey has come a long way politically and economically since achieving independence in 1923. Yet it remains to be seen whether this strategically vital country—a bridge between Asia and Europe, a moderate Muslim nation in the volatile Middle East, a democracy in a region rife with autocrats, an important American ally—will resolve its internal problems and fulfill its potential within the world community.

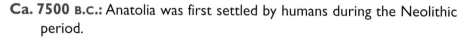
CHRONOLOGY

Ca. 7500 B.C.: Anatolia was first settled by humans during the Neolithic period.

Ca. 1700–1200 B.C.: The Hittites rule the region that is now Turkey.

546 B.C.: The Persians conquer Anatolia.

331 B.C.: Alexander the Great, king of Macedon, defeats the Persians and gains control of Anatolia.

1st century B.C.: Anatolia falls under Roman rule.

A.D. 330: Byzantium, later called Constantinople (today, Istanbul), is made capital of the Roman Empire.

395: The Roman Empire is divided into eastern and western halves. After the fall of the Western Roman Empire in the late fifth century, the Eastern Roman (Byzantine) Empire will survive for 1,000 years.

1071: At the Battle of Manzikert, the Byzantine Empire suffers a crushing defeat at the hands of Seljuk Turks.

1204: Crusaders originally bound for Jerusalem seize Constantinople.

1243: Mongol invaders overrun the Seljuk Empire.

1326: Beginning of the Ottoman Empire.

1453: The Ottoman occupation of Constantinople marks the end of the Byzantine Empire; the Ottomans make the city their capital, renaming it Istanbul.

1520–66: Reign of Süleyman the Magnificent.

1640–48: Reign of Sultan Ibrahim, called "the Debauched," whose deranged actions mark what some consider the lowest point in the era of the Ottoman sultans.

1826: A special army force organized by Sultan Mahmut II destroys the troublesome Janissary corps in a fiery siege of their Constantinople barracks.

1895–96: Ottoman Turks slaughter Armenians in eastern Anatolia.

1908: The Young Turks lead a revolt against the Ottoman government.

1914–18: World War I: The Ottoman Empire allies itself with Germany and ultimately suffers a crushing defeat; during the war the Ottomans undertake a bloody campaign against ethnic Armenians.

1922: A Greek invasion army is repulsed under the leadership of Mustafa Kemal (later named Atatürk).

CHRONOLOGY

1923: The Republic of Turkey is officially formed, with Atatürk as president.

1938: Atatürk dies.

1960–61: The Turkish army temporarily takes control of the government.

1974: Turkish forces are deployed to the island of Cyprus to protect Turkish nationals after a coup by ethnic Greek officers in the Cypriot army.

1980–82: The military once more takes control of the Turkish government; Kenan Evren is elected president in 1982.

1983: Turgut Özal becomes prime minister.

1984: The Kurdistan Workers' Party, or PKK, begins guerrilla attacks within Turkey in an effort to win a Kurdish homeland; the Turkish government responds with brutal force in southeastern Kurdish regions.

1989: Özal becomes Turkey's first president with a nonmilitary background.

1990–91: After Iraq overruns Kuwait, Turkey joins the international alliance opposing Iraq.

1993: Süleyman Demirel becomes president after the death of Özal; Tansu Çiller becomes the nation's first female prime minister.

1996: Necmettin Erbakan becomes Turkey's first Islamist prime minister.

1999: More than 17,000 people are killed in an earthquake in northwestern Turkey; PKK leader Abdullah Öcallan is captured in Kenya and returned to Turkey for trial.

2000: Necdet Sezer becomes president after Süleyman Demirel retires.

2002: The Islamic-based Justice and Development Party wins legislative elections; Turkey lifts the state of emergency in the Kurdish southeast.

2003: A human rights organization alleges continuing use of torture by Turkish police and security forces; Turkey's human rights record must improve for admission into the European Union.

2006: Kurdish protestors clash violently with police in the southeast; an apparent offshoot of the PKK detonates bombs in Istanbul and in tourist resorts, injuring more than 40 people.

2007: Abdullah Gül of the AK Party becomes president amid tension between secularists and Islamists; Turkey launches air strikes against PKK members in Iraq.

2008: Gül visits Armenia and meets with its president, the first Turkish head of state to do so.

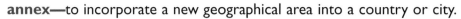

annex—to incorporate a new geographical area into a country or city.

bazaar—a street market, common in the Middle East, with many stalls and shops selling a variety of foods, crafts, fabrics, and other products.

caliph—an Islamic leader, considered the successor of the prophet Muhammad.

coalition government—in a country with a parliamentary system, a government that is formed through a temporary union of two or more political parties or factions, with members of the various parties sharing leadership posts.

concubine—a woman enslaved or chosen to be a man's sexual partner; sultans of the Ottoman Empire kept harems consisting of dozens and even hundreds of concubines.

Crusades—a series of ultimately unsuccessful military campaigns, beginning in 1095 and ending two centuries later, conducted by European Christian armies in attempts to liberate the Holy Land from Muslim control.

cuneiform—a form of writing in ancient western Asia that employed wedge-shaped characters.

dowry—family valuables and property that go with a young woman when she is married.

fez—a traditional flat-topped and brimless hat, often red, that is worn in Arab countries.

gecekondu—flimsy squatter housing on the outskirts of a Turkish city.

genocide—the systematic destruction of a racial or ethnic group.

gross domestic product (GDP)—the total value of all the goods and services a nation produces in a one-year period.

hieroglyphics—any of various ancient systems of writing in which words were represented mainly by pictorial images (of, for example, the sun, an animal, or a house).

imperialism—domination of foreign territories by a distant government.

Janissary—a slave-soldier who was a member of the elite military corps serving the Ottoman sultan.

millets—non-Muslim peoples under the control of the Ottoman Empire who were allowed a measure of local self-rule.

mosque—a Muslim place of prayer.

GLOSSARY

muhtar—the headman of a Turkish village, elected by the residents to represent them to the provincial government.

pagan—a person or society believing in a variety of gods, or in no god.

republican—relating to, or characteristic of, a form of government in which supreme power rests with the body of citizens entitled to vote, who elect leaders to represent them.

scimitar—a large sword with a curved blade used especially by the Ottoman Turks.

Sharia—Islamic law.

steppe—a broad, grassy plain in a semidry region.

sultan—a ruler of the Ottoman Empire.

tawhid—the main principle of Islam, which holds that Allah is the only God.

FURTHER READING

Baralt, Luis A. *Turkey*. New York: Children's Press, 1997.

Barber, Noel. *The Sultans*. New York: Simon and Schuster, 1973.

Bisbee, Eleanor. *The New Turks: Pioneers of the Republic, 1920–1950*. Philadelphia: University of Pennsylvania Press, 1951. Reprint, Westport, Conn.: Greenwood Press, 1975.

Browne, Jane, ed. *Early Civilization*. Secaucus, N.J.: Chartwell Books Inc., 1977.

Campbell, Verity. *Turkey*. 10th ed. Oakland, Calif.: Lonely Planet Publications, 2007.

Clot, André. *Suleiman the Magnificent*. New York: New Amsterdam Books, 1992.

Faroqhi, Suraiya. *Subjects of the Sultans: Culture and Daily Life in the Ottoman Empire*. London: I. B. Tauris & Co., Ltd., 2000.

Feldman, Ruth Tenzer. *The Fall of Constantinople*. Minneapolis: Twenty-First Century Books, 2008.

Howard, Douglas A. *The History of Turkey*. Westport, Conn.: Greenwood Press, 2001.

Kazancigil, Ali, and Ergun Özbudun, eds. *Atatürk: Founder of a Modern State*. Hamden, Conn.: Archon Books, 1981.

Kinzer, Stephen. *Crescent and Star: Turkey Between Two Worlds*. New York: Farrar, Straus and Giroux, 2001.

Kirisci, Kemal, and Gareth M. Winrow. *The Kurdish Question and Turkey: An Example of a Trans-state Ethnic Conflict*. London: Frank Cass & Co., Ltd., 1997.

Metz, Helen Chapin, ed. *Turkey: A Country Study*. Washington, D.C.: Federal Research Division, Library of Congress, 1989.

Miller, Louise R. *Turkey: Between East and West*. New York: Benchmark Books, 1998.

Spencer, William. *The Land and People of Turkey*. New York: J. B. Lippincott, 1990.

Stivachtis, Yannis A., and Meltem Müftüler-Baç, eds. *Turkey-European Relations: Dilemmas, Opportunities, and Constraints*. Lanham, MD: Lexington Books, 2008.

Stoneman, Richard. *A Traveller's History of Turkey*. 3rd ed. New York: Interlink Books, 1998.

Wheatcroft, Andrew. *The Ottomans*. New York: Viking, 1993.

INTERNET RESOURCES

http://www.turkishembassy.org/

The Republic of Turkey's embassy in Washington, D.C.

http://www.mfa.gov.tr

Republic of Turkey, Ministry of Foreign Affairs. Contains information about Turkey generally, and foreign policy information in particular.

http://www.tourismturkey.org

Ministry of Tourism, Turkey. Information about Turkey oriented toward people who are interested in visiting the country.

http://www.historycentral.com/nationbynation/Turkey/index.html

Nation by Nation.com. Basic country information regarding geography, government, history, human rights, and so on.

http://www.cia.gov/library/publications/the-world-factbook/geos/tu.html

CIA—The World Factbook. Current country statistics and general information at the website of the U.S. Central Intelligence Agency.

http://www.turkey.com

One of the numerous country sites operated by Virtual Countries, Inc.

http://travel.state.gov/travel/cis_pa_tw/cis/cis_1046.html

Turkey: Consular Information Sheet. Provided by the U.S. Department of State, this page gives details about travel requirements and provides travel advisories.

http://www.gksoft.com/govt/en/tr.html

Governments on the WWW: Turkey. Provides Web links to many Turkish government agencies, political parties, world embassies, and other Internet resources.

http://www.lonelyplanet.com/destinations/middle_east/turkey

Lonely Planet WorldGuide: Turkey. Travel-related information about Turkey, with background material on history, culture, and the environment.

http://www.worldtravelguide.net/data/tur/tur.asp

WorldTravelGuide.Net. A wealth of country information maintained by Columbus Publishing.

INDEX

Numbers in **bold italic** refer to captions.

INDEX

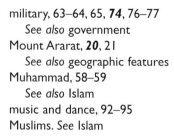

INDEX

INDEX

2:	© OTTN Publishing	61:	Timothy A. Clary/AFP/Getty Images
3:	Turkish Tourist Office	65:	Staton R. Winter/Getty Images
12:	Turkish Tourist Office	66:	Turkish Tourist Office
16:	Turkish Tourist Office	69:	© OTTN Publishing
19:	© OTTN Publishing	71:	AFP/Corbis
20:	Adam Woolfitt/Corbis	72:	Turkish Tourist Office
23:	Turkish Tourist Office	73:	Turkish Tourist Office
25:	Turkish Tourist Office	74:	Staton R. Winter/Getty Images
28:	Chris Hellier/Corbis	79:	Bettmann/Corbis
32:	Turkish Tourist Office	82:	Turkish Tourist Office
33:	Hulton Archive/Getty Images	84:	Turkish Tourist Office
34:	Bettmann/Corbis	87:	Turkish Tourist Office
37:	Réunion des Museés Nationaux/Art Resource, NY	89:	Turkish Tourist Office
38:	Erich Lessing/Art Resource, NY	90:	Turkish Tourist Office
41:	© OTTN Publishing	91:	Turkish Tourist Office
42:	Historical Picture Archive/Corbis	93:	Turkish Tourist Office
47:	Hulton Archive/Getty Images	94:	Turkish Tourist Office
49:	Adam Woolfitt/Corbis	96:	David Turnley/Corbis
50:	John Levy/Liaison/Getty Images	99:	Scott Peterson/Liaison/Getty Images
52:	Staton R. Winter/Liaison/Getty Images	101:	Photo. No. AR 7558-B in the John F. Kennedy Library, Boston
53:	© OTTN Publishing	104:	U.S. Department of Defense
56:	Scott Peterson/Liaison/Getty Images	106:	Eslami Rad/Liaison/Getty Images
59:	AFP/Corbis		

Cover photo: PhotoDisc

CONTRIBUTORS

The **FOREIGN POLICY RESEARCH INSTITUTE (FPRI)** served as editorial consultants for the MAJOR MUSLIM NATIONS series. FPRI is one of the nation's oldest "think tanks." The Institute's Middle East Program focuses on Gulf security, monitors the Arab-Israeli peace process, and sponsors an annual conference for teachers on the Middle East, plus periodic briefings on key developments in the region.

Among the FPRI's trustees is a former Secretary of State and a former Secretary of the Navy (and among the FPRI's former trustees and interns, two current Undersecretaries of Defense), not to mention two university presidents emeritus, a foundation president, and several active or retired corporate CEOs.

The scholars of FPRI include a former aide to three U.S. Secretaries of State, a Pulitzer Prize–winning historian, a former president of Swarthmore College and a Bancroft Prize–winning historian, and two former staff members of the National Security Council. And the FPRI counts among its extended network of scholars—especially its Inter-University Study Groups—representatives of diverse disciplines, including political science, history, economics, law, management, religion, sociology, and psychology.

DR. HARVEY SICHERMAN is president and director of the Foreign Policy Research Institute in Philadelphia, Pennsylvania. He has extensive experience in writing, research, and analysis of U.S. foreign and national security policy, both in government and out. He served as Special Assistant to Secretary of State Alexander M. Haig Jr. and as a member of the Policy Planning Staff of Secretary of State James A. Baker III. Dr. Sicherman was also a consultant to Secretary of the Navy John F. Lehman Jr. (1982–1987) and Secretary of State George Shultz (1988).

A graduate of the University of Scranton (B.S., History, 1966), Dr. Sicherman earned his Ph.D. at the University of Pennsylvania (Political Science, 1971), where he received a Salvatori Fellowship. He is author or editor of numerous books and articles, including *America the Vulnerable: Our Military Problems and How to Fix Them* (FPRI, 2002) and *Palestinian Autonomy, Self-Government and Peace* (Westview Press, 1993). He edits *Peacefacts*, an FPRI bulletin that monitors the Arab-Israeli peace process.

DANIEL E. HARMON is an author and editor in Spartanburg, South Carolina. He has written more than 30 nonfiction books, one short story collection, and numerous magazine and newspaper articles. Harmon has served for many years as associate editor of *Sandlapper: The Magazine of South Carolina* and editor of *The Lawyer's PC*, a national computer newsletter published by West Group. His special interests include nautical history and folk music.